The
German
Americans

By Diane Yancey

LUCENT BOOKS

An imprint of Thomson Gale, a part of The Thomson Corporation

Detroit • New York • San Francisco • San Diego • New Haven, Conn. • Waterville, Maine • London • Munich

LIBRARY OF CONGRESS CATALOGING-IN-PUBLICATION DATA

Yancey, Diane.
  The German Americans / by Diane Yancey.
    p. cm. — (Immigrants in America)
  Includes bibliographical references and index.
  Summary: Life in the old country—The voyage to America—All ashore!—Newcomers in a new world—Real Americans—A powerful force—"Foreign malcontents and misfits"—Remembering a proud heritage.
  ISBN 1-56006-962-7 (hard cover : alk. paper) 1. German Americans—History—Juvenile literature. 2. Immigrants—United States—History—Juvenile literature. 3. Germany—Emigration and immigration—History—Juvenile literature. 4. United States—Emigration and immigration—History—Juvenile literature. I. Title. II. Series.
  E184.G3Y36 2005
  973'.0431—dc22
                                                                    2004023422

CONTENTS

FOREWORD

Immigrants have come to America at different times, for different reasons, and from many different places. They leave their homelands to escape religious and political persecution, poverty, war, famine, and countless other hardships. The journey is rarely easy. Sometimes, it entails a long and hazardous ocean voyage. Other times, it follows a circuitous route through refugee camps and foreign countries. At the turn of the twentieth century, for instance, Italian peasants, fleeing poverty, boarded steamships bound for New York, Boston, and other eastern seaports. And during the 1970s and 1980s, Vietnamese men, women, and children, victims of a devastating war, began arriving at refugee camps in Arkansas, Pennsylvania, Florida, and California, en route to establishing new lives in the United States.

Whatever the circumstances surrounding their departure, the immigrants' journey is always made more difficult by the knowledge that they leave behind family, friends, and a familiar way of life. Despite this, immigrants continue to come to America because, for many, the United States represents something they could not find at home: freedom and opportunity for themselves and their children.

No matter what their reasons for emigrating, where they have come from, or when they left, once here, nearly all immigrants face considerable challenges in adapting and making the United States

their new home. Language barriers, unfamiliar surroundings, and sometimes hostile neighbors make it difficult for immigrants to assimilate into American society. Some Vietnamese, for instance, could not read or write in their native tongue when they arrived in the United States. This heightened their struggle to communicate with employers who demanded they be literate in English, a language vastly different from their own. Likewise, Irish immigrant schoolchildren in Boston faced classmates who teased and belittled their lilting accent. Immigrants from Russia often felt isolated, having settled in areas of the United States where they had no access to traditional Russian foods. Similarly, Italian families, used to certain wines and spices, rarely shopped or traveled outside of New York's Little Italy, a self-contained community cut off from the rest of the city.

Even when first-generation immigrants do successfully settle into life in the United States, their children, born in America, often have different values and are influenced more by their country of birth than their parents' traditions. Children want to be a part of the American culture and usually welcome American ideals, beliefs, and styles. As they become more Americanized—adopting Western dating habits and fashions, for instance—they tend to cast aside or even actively reject the traditions embraced by their parents. Assimilation, then, often becomes an ideological dispute that creates conflict among immigrants of every ethnicity. Whether Chinese, Italian, Russian, or Vietnamese, young people battle their elders for respect, individuality, and freedom, issues that often would not have come up in their homeland. And no matter how tightly the first generations hold on to their traditions, in the end, it is usually the young people who decide what to keep and what to discard.

The Immigrants in America series fully examines the immigrant experience. Each book in the series discusses why the immigrants left their homeland, what the journey to America was like, what they experienced when they arrived, and the challenges of assimilation. Each volume includes discussion of triumph and tragedy, contributions and influences, history and the future. Fully documented primary and secondary source quotations enliven the text. Sidebars highlight interesting events and personalities. Annotated bibliographies offer ideas for additional research. Each book in this dynamic series provides students with a wealth of information as well as launching points for further discussion.

Three Hundred Years of Immigration

From colonial governor Peter Minuit, who purchased the island of Manhattan from local Native Americans for twenty-four dollars in 1626, to Secretary of State Henry Kissinger, who negotiated the end of the Vietnam War in 1973, German immigrants and their descendants have made distinct and enduring marks on American culture. They have settled in every part of the United States and represent every level of society. They have helped shape American life and became a part of it in unique ways.

German products have become standards in American homes—Hershey's chocolate, Spreckels sugar, and Folger's coffee to name but three. German words —*delicatessen, glitz, kaput, spritz*, and *zigzag*—have become a part of everyday conversation. Towns with names like New Braunfels, Fredericksburg, and King of Prussia serve as reminders of German settlers who lived in them. German contributions in the fields of education, agriculture, science, and the arts have helped the United States reach and maintain the position and prestige it has enjoyed for the past two hundred years.

Colonial Times

Unlike many other ethnic groups, German immigrants came to America in several waves that spanned the course of three hundred years. The first wave—before 1700—was relatively small and was made up primarily of those seeking religious freedom in the New World. The most famous of these was a band of thirteen families from the village of Krefeld in western Germany who arrived on the sailing ship *Concord*—later known as "the German *Mayflower*"—in 1683. Despite the fact that their leader, Francis Daniel Pastorius, was young and a scholar, he proved wise enough to choose a good location for their new settlement, which was located near Philadelphia, Pennsylvania. Pastorius wrote of it in 1700, "As relating to our newly laid out town, *Germanopolis*, or Germantown, it is situated on a deep and very fertile soil, and is blessed with an abundance of fine springs and fountains of fresh water. The main street is sixty and the cross street forty feet in width. Every family has a plot of ground for yard and garden three acres in size." [1]

Germantown flourished as time passed and was known for being more peaceful and prosperous than any other such settlement in North America. Records show that few crimes were committed there, and those crimes were minor ones. One recorded instance involved a man named Caspar Karsten, who was called before the judge for being disrespectful to a policeman. Another involved a man named Muller who was charged with having made an illegal bet, wagering that he could smoke one hundred pipes of tobacco in a single day.

German Americans like this delicatessen owner have been an integral part of American society for over three centuries.

Modern Germany

during the peak immigration years of 1846 to 1892, more than 100,000 German newcomers arrived annually. Three times—in 1854, 1881, and 1882—there were more than 200,000 arrivals per year. In the 1880s alone, more than 1.5 million Germans migrated to America.

This great wave of people left Germany for a variety of reasons. Some were personal and included boredom, trouble with the law, and bad relationships with other family members. Sixteen-year-old Wilhelm Burkert, for instance, was sent away by his strict stepmother after he committed a small juvenile offense that was probably linked to the use of alcohol.

Most reasons were more universal, however. Many emigrated (left Germany) to avoid religious oppression. Some wanted to escape poverty and political subjugation. Others were drawn by reports of riches and adventure. Author Philip Taylor observes:

> [Some came to America out of a] desire to escape family or citizen's obligations, for personal disappointments, for ambition, optimism, or despair. People moved when . . . they decided that the way of life they wanted, whether viewed as a standard of living or a good society or a

Germans continued to arrive in America throughout the 1700s and early 1800s. Many of them settled in Pennsylvania and became known as the Pennsylvania Dutch. Most engaged in farming, at which they were extremely successful. For the most part they maintained their own language and customs, with the family and the church being central to their lives. The Pennsylvania Dutch language, a mixture of South German and English, is the oldest immigrant language still in use in the United States today.

The Great Wave

Though the impact of the German immigrants during this early period was considerable, the great era of German immigration began after the Napoleonic Wars (1799–1815) in Europe. Eighteen times godly congregation, could better be promoted by going to America than by staying at home. [2]

German immigrant backgrounds and lifestyles were quite varied. Many were farmers and craftspersons. Others were pastors, doctors, lawyers, and intellectuals. The overwhelming majority was poor, but the wealthy made the journey as well. Upon arrival, most gathered in large cities, then spread out across the country. They were instrumental in settling the plains states—Iowa, Nebraska, the Dakotas, and

A Shrewd Businessman

Although Peter Minuit worked for the Dutch in America, he was German and had the common sense and frugality that characterized many German immigrants. The following short biography, entitled "About Peter Minuit," can be read in full on the Daughters of the American Revolution Web site at www.molsk.com/dar/minuit.html.

Peter Minuit is best known as the man who bought the island of Manhattan from the Indians for the legendary sum of 60 Dutch guilders, or $24.00. Born in Wesel, Germany, in 1580, Minuit was a Walloon (a Belgian, French-speaking Protestant) whose family fled persecution at the hands of the Spanish army and settled in the Netherlands. He was an employee of the Dutch West India Company, which held a monopoly over all Dutch trade with West Africa and the Americas. . . .

On May 4, 1626, Minuit arrived at the mouth of the Hudson River to take up his assignment as the third director of the New Netherland Colony, the Dutch settlement centered at the southern tip of Manhattan that was established in 1624. The colonists traded furs with the local native peoples—Mahicans and Lenapes—and set to work farming the area bounded by the Delaware and Connecticut rivers and the west bank of the Hudson, including outposts on what are known today as Staten Island and Governors Island. . . .

To solidify control over the island, Peter Minuit purchased Manhattan from the Lenapes for 60 guilders' worth of trade goods. No deed or bill of sale has survived . . . but the similar purchase of Staten Island was paid by him and five other colonists in duffel cloth, kettles, axes, hoes, wampum [beads or shells used as money], drilling awls, "Jew's Harps" [small musical instruments] and "diverse other wares."

Peter Minuit served as director of New Netherland until 1633. . . . He died in 1638, reportedly drowned at sea during a hurricane.

others. There, they established farms and businesses, and, in the words of historian Oscar Handlin, "helped to bring the promised but undeveloped land in which they arrived into a place of prominence in the world." [3]

Although improved conditions in Germany led to a decrease in emigration for a time after 1890, Nazi oppression, war, and Communist aggression again drove Germans to emigrate during the twentieth century. Following World War II nearly a million arrived in the United States, especially during the 1950s. They, too, hoped to escape the problems associated with economic, social, and political reconstruction in their homeland and to find a better life in America.

Opposition and Assimilation

German immigrants were not perfect. They had some beliefs and behaviors that Americans considered offensive—an allegiance to radical politics and a love of beer drinking being two of them—and they faced prejudice and rejection at various points throughout their years in America. Through it all, however, their determination to become accepted as real Americans remained strong. In fact, many so underplayed their German heritage that it was virtually forgotten within a generation or two. Authors Nathan Glazer and Daniel P. Moynihan call the phenomenon an "ethnic disappearance."

They stated in 1963, "The Germans as a *group* are vanished. No appeals are made to the German vote, there are no German politicians . . . and generally speaking, no German component in the structure of the ethnic interests of the city. The logical explanation of this development . . . is simply that the Germans have been 'assimilated.' " [4]

Yet as a result of the millions of German immigrants who arrived in the United States during the nineteenth century, persons with German ancestry make up the largest ethnic group in the United States today. An estimated 43 million, more than one in six Americans, are descendants of German immigrants. Only recently, as a result of America's new-found emphasis on different ethnicities, some of them have become curious about their German roots. They have delved into the reasons their ancestors came to the United States, have learned of the travails they endured on the trip over, and have begun to appreciate the challenges they overcame when they arrived. All those experiences, which make up the rich and fascinating history that is the legacy of the German immigrants, have added to their insight and understanding of themselves. And, as noted by one of their descendants, Robert E. Ward, president of the German-American Historical Association of Cuyahoga County, Ohio: "Whether born here or abroad, we are extremely proud of our heritage." [5]

CHAPTER ONE

Life in the Old Country

More than 3 million Germans who immigrated to America between 1845 and 1890 were driven by unhappiness with conditions in their homeland and were lured by dreams of riches and a fresh start in a new land. Most were poor and wanted to improve their economic situation. Others had heard of political and religious freedom—something they lacked in the old country—and wanted to take advantage of that. Author Willi Paul Adams observes, "Whether 'push factors,' fanned by disgruntlement with living conditions in Germany, or whether 'pull factors'—faith in more favorable opportunities in the United States—exercised a greater influence on the emigrant's decision to leave, is im-

possible to ascertain." [6] Regardless of the reasons they chose to leave, most retained ties to their homeland based on personal attachments and a deep-seated love of their culture and traditions.

War and Repression

In the 1840s, when the vast tide of Germans began migrating to America, Germany was not the united democracy that it is today. Instead, it was a collection of thirty-nine nation-states that included Prussia, Saxony, Bavaria, Bohemia, and many others. These states were headed by noble families who ruled with unlimited power, setting laws according to their own will. They could ban some members of

German Confederation, 1815-1866

Boundary of the Confederation

War of Austrian Succession (1740–1748), the Seven Years' War (1756–1763), and the Napoleonic Wars (1799–1815).

Normal life was continually being disrupted by all the warfare. Cities were destroyed. Villages were burned. Farms were wiped out. Large numbers of men were killed in battle. Women and children were left to survive as best they could. Historian Gerhard Rempel observes of the Thirty Years' War, "The real losers in the war were the German people. Over 300,000 had been killed in battle. Millions of civilians had died of malnutrition and disease, and wandering, undisciplined troops had robbed, burned, and looted almost at will." [7]

the population from certain occupations and limit who and when others could marry. They could set taxes so high that families could not afford to buy necessities such as seeds to plant their crops or meat to put on the table. They could draft men into the army and send them to war at a moment's notice.

These rulers and others throughout Europe were always interested in gaining more power and settling grievances against neighboring kingdoms, so wars had been common occurrences in the past. The Thirty Years' War (1618–1648) was the longest and most devastating of these conflicts. Others included the War of Spanish Succession (1701–1714), the

Not only did members of the aristocracy have the power of life and death over their subjects, but they dictated how everyone worshipped as well. Rulers who were members of the Roman Catholic Church established Catholicism as the official religion of their states and expected their subjects to be obedient to its teachings. At the same time, Protestant rulers belonging to either the Lutheran or the Calvinist Churches compelled their subjects to conform to that sect's beliefs. Minority religious sects such as Jews, Quakers, and Mennonites (a Christian group that rejected infant baptism and believed in the separation of church and state, in the shunning of nonbelievers, and in simplicity of life) were considered heretics and were routinely persecuted. To escape discrimination, thousands fled to America over the centuries, taking advantage of new religious opportunities and paving the way for other German immigrants who would follow in later years. Richard O' Connor observes, "[They] were united in one determination: not to be ruled by kings or princelings from across the sea. More than any of the other nationalities in the wilderness of the New World they had cut themselves loose from ties that might have bound them to Europe." [8]

The Forty-Eighters

Under the oppressive hand of noble rulers, even peaceful years were not easy times for ordinary Germans. Everyone worked hard, either farming or making goods such as shoes, candles, barrels, and the like in their homes. Houses were small, dark, and smoky from wood fires that were used for cooking and heating. Medical care was crude. Education was considered extremely

Anti-Semitism

In addition to Mennonites and other minority religious groups, German Jews also endured religious persecution in Germany. From earliest times, European Christians looked on them with suspicion and blamed them for the killing of Jesus. Jews were believed to be disloyal, untrustworthy, and devious, and they were often accused of such activities as poisoning wells, ritually murdering children, and blighting crops.

At the time of the largest wave of German immigration to America, most German Jews were assimilated into German society and were loyal to their country. Nevertheless, they often faced repression and restrictions on their lives. They were denied citizenship, were prohibited from holding some jobs, and were heavily taxed. At times their lives were in jeopardy when anti-Semitic (anti-Jewish) feelings erupted into violence.

When conditions became unbearable, or when an opportunity arose that offered brighter prospects, many packed their belongings and emigrated. America proved a haven for many over the years. Ironically, America's tight anti-immigration policies during the 1930s prevented many German Jews from entering the United States when they were most desperate. While Adolf Hitler imprisoned and killed millions of their numbers, only about three hundred thousand German Jews were permitted to enter the United States between 1933 and 1943.

valuable, but good schools were expensive, and village schools provided only a basic education. Many people could barely read or write. Although few people had the time or opportunity to outwardly rebel against their bleak, powerless existence, many of them yearned for a better life. One writer observed, "There are many restrictions, and the young, the restless, and the imaginative thirst for their ideal freedom." [9]

The yearning changed to vocal protests in about 1840. Word began spreading that in countries such as England, France, and the United States, governments recognized and respected the rights of ordinary people. In those countries, white males were allowed to vote and to have some say in the laws that governed their lives.

As a result, some progressive Germans—teachers, professors, and other intellectuals—began pushing for the creation of constitutional governments that would give citizens greater rights. When they realized that German rulers had no intention of giving them a voice in government, the reformers revolted. Known as the "Forty-Eighters" for the year of their uprising, they took to the streets, demanding democracy, a fair tax system, freedom of the press, and an elected government that would be responsible to a parliament.

The revolutionaries were sincere in their cause, but from the beginning they quarreled among themselves. Conservatives, liberals, and moderates could not agree on whether the new Germany should be a monarchy, a republic, a loose federation of states, or a unified nation. Power struggles between political and regional groups quickly led to an abandonment of the original revolutionary program. The revolution itself failed after state militias forced the reformers to disband.

Disillusioned and afraid of government vengeance, about ten thousand revolutionaries, including feminist Mathilde Anneke, future civil war commander Franz Sigel, and future secretary of state Carl Schurz, fled the country. America—the land of liberty—was their destination of choice.

In 1848 government soldiers cut down a group of revolutionaries in a square in Berlin.

America, the Bountiful

Articles and books written in the mid-1800s by German author Gottfried Duden played a significant role in convincing Germans to immigrate to the United States. In his book The German-Americans, *historian Richard O'Connor provides background on Duden and his enthusiasm for America.*

Duden wrote glowingly of his everyday experiences on the Middle Western farm. One article would relate the hard but rewarding labor of clearing a patch of forest—that there was virgin soil, not that which had been worked for centuries, was enthralling in itself to Germans—and another would tell of bringing in the bountiful harvest. Others dwelled almost poetically on the forests which enclosed every farm . . . and on the rivers flowing through the wilderness, the majesty of western sunsets and the overwhelming effulgence [radiance] of moonlight, but little mention of hard winters or spring floods or steaming summers. He also remarked frequently on the absence of overbearing princes and clergymen, strutting soldiers and ruthless tax collectors (a farm large enough to keep eight horses was taxed only twelve dollars annually), but passed over the crudity of frontier manners and the frequent brutality of the frontiersmen.

Schurz expressed his feelings at the time he emigrated: "Where to go? America, I told myself . . . Ubi libertas, ibi patria [Where liberty is, there is my country]." [10]

Despite the revolution's failure, political change for Germany was in the near future. In 1871 Germany officially became one nation under the rule of King Wilhelm I and Chancellor (prime minister) Otto von Bismarck. Although Bismarck encouraged nationalism and industrialization, his militaristic policies, as well as his *Kulturkampf* ("culture struggle") against the Roman Catholic Church, again caused many Germans to emigrate to avoid military service and religious persecution.

The Industrial Revolution

Political and religious turmoil motivated some Germans to emigrate, but economic change was the strongest reason why millions of Germans left their homeland in the 1800s. The Industrial Revolution—the widespread replacement of manual labor by machines—was at least partially responsible for that wave of emigration.

The Industrial Revolution began in England in about 1800, after Scottish inventor James Watt developed a steam engine that could be used to power equipment such as mechanical looms used in making textiles. As a result of this advance, factories replaced home

This nineteenth-century woodcut shows the deplorable living conditions of a shantytown near Berlin. As one family works a small plot of land, children beg from a wealthy couple.

workshops, and cities grew as people moved from rural areas to find work.

As the Industrial Revolution reached Germany, a similar population shift occurred. Cities such as Hamburg, Berlin, and Nuremberg became industrial centers where products such as paper, china, leather products, clocks, and jewelry were made. The development of machinery and railway systems brought about an increased demand for coal and steel; as a result, coal-producing districts like the Ruhr, the Saar, and Upper Silesia were transformed from agricultural to industrial regions.

"Eat Grass"

Such progress provided additional job opportunities, but with large numbers of the population looking for work, competition was intense. Employers discovered that they could pay low wages and ignore

working conditions because there was always someone willing to take the available jobs. As a result, men and women had to work more than fifteen hours a day, six days a week, in order to make just enough money to survive. With no child labor laws, even young children had to join the workforce.

A family's combined wages bought only the cheapest food, such as bread and potatoes, and barely covered the rent on a ramshackle tenement house or cottage that had no running water or sanitary facilities. In cities, families lived together under the most crowded conditions, as researcher Else Conrad writes of one Munich family with four children:

> Around the room, the wife was busy cooking; next to her stood the laundry vat, filled with children's laundry; on the clothes line, spanned through the

room, cleaned laundry, still wet, was hanging. . . . Two children who do not yet attend school were playing on the floor, on a bench in front of the window the husband, presently out of employment, was sitting, idle. [11]

Under such unhealthy conditions, multitudes died of diseases such as typhoid, dysentery, tuberculosis, and cholera. Children who survived infancy usually suffered from malnutrition and tooth decay. There were no government protections such as social security or health insurance, and protests to employers about living conditions usually failed. For instance, when weavers in the region of Silesia demanded a raise in their starvation wages in June 1844, they were told by unsympathetic employers "to eat grass," [12] and their revolt was put down by the Prussian army.

Betrayed by the Land

Farmers and other country folk lived in poverty, too, just as they had for generations. Like their counterparts in the city, their homes were tiny one- or two-room cottages with no indoor plumbing. They slept on straw mattresses, usually laid on the floor. They drank milk and ate dark bread and vegetables—potatoes, turnips, onions, and the like. Historian Walter D. Kamphoefner notes:

Breakfast usually consisted of a few slices of pumpernickel and coffee made from roasted chicory and only occasionally real coffee beans; for lunch there was sometimes stew made of vegetables but more often potatoes or sour milk; and then bread and coffee were served again for supper. Meat was seldom or never seen on the table in most homes. [13]

Periodic crop failure was one reason for such poverty. In 1844, for instance, a potato blight that struck Ireland swept across parts of Germany as well. The majority of German farmers did not grow potatoes as their sole crop, but some—such as those in the Eifel and Mosel districts in northwestern Germany—did. As their crops turned black and rotted before they could be sold or eaten, families lost everything they had and became destitute. The magistrate of the town of Trier reported, "Adverse circumstances and poor harvests have befallen the farmers in this area . . . in recent years. Many of them have fallen into grinding poverty and debt as a result." [14]

Poor harvests were not the only problem. The rich owned most of the agricultural land, leaving many families with no option but to work as tenants on large estates. They paid rent as well as supported themselves by trying to grow crops on small plots of land that were depleted of nutrients. Some commoners owned their own land, but their farms were small as a result of having been divided among male children for many generations. At times, plots were so tiny that a family could not grow enough food to support itself.

Some regions in northern Germany had avoided this problem by requiring that farms be passed on to one heir—usually a firstborn son—rather than be divided.

Hardworking German immigrants, like these farmers in Nebraska, encouraged family members and friends back home to join them in America.

That meant, however, that other siblings could work their family's land only as farmhands, or they could settle for a small amount of money as their part of the inheritance and go out to find work elsewhere. In the mid-1800s many young Germans used their inheritances to buy one-way tickets to America, reportedly a land of opportunity where one could easily support oneself and one's family.

The Friends-and-Relatives Effect

As the 1800s wore on, many ordinary Germans were lured by the thought of a better life in America. They were working hard, but they were losing ground both economically and socially. They were not yet penniless, but their future looked bleak. Artisans who had once taken pride in being independent business owners had compromised and taken factory positions. Farmers who had owned land for genera-

tions had to forfeit some or all of it to pay taxes and had become *Kotters*, or tenant farmers. As one worker, Moritz Bromme, noted at the time, providing even the basics for one's family was extremely difficult: "This week [my daughter] Heddel's shoes will be soled, [my son] Ernst's soles are worn down, they have to be done, and Walter does not even have shoes. Then all of them need indoor shoes, and we urgently need a bed. . . . To sleep with three persons in one bed is no sleep at all." [15]

In contrast to life in Germany, conditions in America sounded attractive. There, according to reliable reports, land was fertile and sometimes free for the taking. Jobs were plentiful, and ordinary people could live comfortably and even prosper.

Many Germans learned of these conditions from relatives who had gone to America years earlier. In letters home, these forerunners wrote glowing reports of their new homeland. One man, J.K. Meidenbauer, wrote to his sister from his new home in Wisconsin, "You will next ask: is it really good in America? . . . and I can give you the answer, from my full conviction . . . Yes, it is really good here. I would advise my sister Barbara to come over with her intended [fiancé] for she can do better than in Germany. There are no dues, no titles here, no taxes . . . no (mounted) police, no beggars." [16]

To some, the most exciting part of America was the unrestricted freedom that everyone enjoyed. Johann Bauer, a successful immigrant farmer, wrote to his parents in 1868, "The greatest [advantage in America] is that you can be more independent than there, that you can start something today, and if you're not happy or satisfied you can start something else tomorrow and without

making a stir. That is the main thing that makes America so dear to people, the freedom of movement." [17]

Stories about the good life in America spread quickly. As a result, in some areas chain migrations—sometimes called "the friends-and-relatives effect"—took place. One family who had gone before encouraged others to immigrate; they in turn encouraged others to come, and so forth. Financial assistance made the move more attractive as well. Author Timothy J. Hatton writes, "Once established, channels of migration perpetuated themselves through earlier migrants providing pre-paid tickets for the passage, providing food and shelter to newly arrived friends and relatives and using social networks to gain access to job opportunities." [18]

An early-twentieth-century advertisement featuring the Statue of Liberty promises European immigrants a chance for a better life in America.

The Lure of Something Better

In addition to family and friends, there were agencies that did their best to persuade Germans to immigrate to America, too. The Northern Pacific Railway, for example, tried to attract settlers to such areas as Minnesota in the 1870s. Using brochures and human representatives in Germany, it praised the territory's climate, rich soil, schools, and churches. It also promised 160 acres of free land to those who met the qualifications set down by the Homestead Act of 1862.

Some state and territorial governments set up departments of immigration in order to promote their areas. Minnesota Territory's first commissioner of immigration, Eugene Burnand, advertised the region through pamphlets, immigrant newspapers, and persuasive speeches made to newly arrived immigrants at the ship docks. Colorado promoted its farming, stock raising, mining, and other opportunities in brochures it distributed in Germany. One read:

> The poor should come to Colorado, because here they can by industry and frugality better their condition. The rich should come here, because they can more advantageously invest their means than in any other region. The young should come here to get an early start on the road to wealth, and the old should come to get a new lease on life, and to enjoy their declining years in a country unequalled for its natural beauty and loveliness. [19]

German books and magazine articles also sparked interest and enthusiasm with their descriptions of immigrant life. The works of author Gottfried Duden were among the most influential because Duden was well known, had occupied an important position in the Prussian civil service, and was considered trustworthy. Duden traveled to America in 1824 and returned to Germany in 1829 to write of his experiences. His best-selling book, *Report on a Journey to the Western States of North America*, contained descriptions of America's beautiful countryside, its democratic institutions, and its people's comfortable lifestyles. "[In America] the whole family lives carefree and happily without a single piece of ready money," Duden wrote, referring to what he termed a typical farm family. Duden also suggested that, if a family settled in the South and embraced the institution of slavery, "he [the owner] can confine himself entirely to duties of inspection without laying his own hand to anything; and the housewife will have just as little to complain of in the work of the household." [20]

The thought of land and leisure time was very attractive to Germans who were tired of working hard and getting nowhere. They had little money to risk on gambles, but for many the payoff seemed too good to ignore. Thus, many made their plans, purchased their tickets, and set off for the ships that would carry them to a new life.

CHAPTER TWO

The Voyage to America

Germans who made the decision to immigrate to America faced a long, difficult journey across the ocean. However, the voyage was only one part. Leaving familiar surroundings to step into the unknown was frightening, particularly for those who had never been farther than the local village. Faced with the complications of travel, many wondered if they would ever reach their destination. The delays and transfers that emigrant Johann Pritzlaff experienced after traveling by wagon across Germany to reach the port of Hamburg were common to many. He recalled, "As of today we have been in Ham-

burg already for 4 weeks. We will travel by steamship to Hull in England, from there to Liverpool [England] by steamboat, then we have to go by sailing ship and will perhaps land in Philadelphia." [21]

Preparing to Depart

For many, deciding to emigrate involved a great deal of discussion. Those who considered the move usually asked advice from parents, sisters, brothers, aunts, uncles, friends, and anyone else in their village or neighborhood who mattered. All aspects of the proposed migration were discussed—costs, sacrifices, benefits, and

European immigrants on their way to America crowd the deck of an Atlantic liner. The transatlantic voyage was very difficult for most immigrants.

the impact on loved ones both short and long term. Most family members were supportive of the migrant's adventure, but some were angry and resentful, seeing the move as desertion of kindred as well as homeland.

Once the decision to go was made, preparations began in earnest. Everyone making the trip had to obtain, fill out, and submit an application to the government for emigration. This could be denied if one had a criminal history or if authorities believed someone was trying to avoid military service. Those who had debts or owed back taxes could also be refused permission to leave until their records were cleared.

Ticket purchases were often made about this time. Travelers who had the money to engage a first- or second-class cabin on one of the upper decks of a ship usually waited to purchase tickets at the ship itself, but those who planned to travel in third class, known as steerage, had more options. Offices selling steerage tickets were located in cities throughout the country, and freelance agents also traveled from village to village selling "packages" that included the cost of overland travel to a port in Germany, passage on a ship to a port in Britain or another European country (if necessary), the transatlantic passage, and overland transportation to the final destination in the United States.

Prepaid tickets eliminated the problem of inflation, which often upset the plans of those who waited to buy their tickets at a port. During peak travel times, when space on ships was in high demand, ticket prices could skyrocket. Poor travelers often found they could no longer afford to travel. As a result, some had to delay their trips until they could find work and earn the additional funds. Carl Berthold, who emigrated in 1852, wrote to his family from the port of Bremerhaven:

The cost of passage is going up every day. We were very glad that we had signed up, otherwise we would have had to pay 40 talers [about 28 dollars] in gold. . . . We want to advise everyone who wants to go to America to sign up at home . . . for there were several here who thought they could cross for 28 talers [about 20 dollars] and didn't have any more, either, so could do nothing but return to their homeland again. [22]

By the late nineteenth century, up to one-third of emigrants traveled on prepaid tickets that had been sent by relatives in the United States. This was usually because those in America were better off than those in Germany and also could choose when the time was right to welcome new arrivals.

Sailing in Luxury

Shipping companies did their best to attract customers during the years of heavy immigration, sometimes making their ships sound like luxury hotels. Such was the case in the following advertisement for the Hamburg-American Packet Company, whose ships regularly ran between Hamburg and New York. The ad can be found in Lois Jones's online article "To America" at www.cochems.com/history/ch8_to_america.html.

The Company's Ocean Steamers have been constructed by the most famous engineers and iron ship-builders in Europe. . . . The commodious staterooms are all on the same main deck, thus insuring those greatest luxuries at sea—perfect ventilation and light. . . . The steerage is situated directly below the main deck. It is spacious, light and well ventilated, and has separate compartments for single men, women and families. An efficient corps of stewards and servants, speaking several languages, is ready . . . to attend to the wants of passengers. . . . The Hamburg Mail Line has always enjoyed an enviable reputation for the excellent fare provided for its patrons, the menu served not being surpassed by the best hotels either in Europe or America.

After packing up their belongings, German immigrants then began the long journey to a port city.

Last Farewells

With a date set for departure, land, animals, and anything else that could not be carried were sold or given to relatives who were staying behind. Bedding, clothing, valuables, and sentimental items were usually taken along. Although shipping lines often provided food on board, some families carried their own food, dishes, and cooking pots for the voyage as well.

The most painful and emotional part of this stage of the journey was saying goodbye to family and friends. America was four thousand miles away; an unimaginable distance before the days of jet travel. Partings were often considered final, as a member of the Schuette family, who left Germany for Wisconsin in 1848, explained: "The neighbors and friends were on hand to say a last farewell and tears flowed in profusion (since) anyone leaving for America was considered about to pass into eternity." [23]

After the farewells, the first stage of the journey—getting to a port city—began. Many travelers set off from home on foot or in horse-drawn wagons and took days or weeks to get to the coast, which could be hundreds of miles away. Those who lived near a river usually traveled by boat or barge. After railroad lines began crisscrossing the country in about 1830, anyone who could afford it took the train. Many used a combination of means. For instance, Johann Bauer began his trip from Mannheim on the Rhine River, traveling by steamboat to the city of Cologne. He then transferred to a train to finish his journey to the port of Bremen.

The Perils of Hamburg

Bauer began his ocean voyage in Bremen, but more than 1 million emigrants left Germany from Hamburg, the region's largest port, between 1836 and 1880. Like all large cities, the port was a hazardous place for emigrants, many of whom were simple country people. They were unprepared for the swindlers, con men, and other unscrupulous individuals who lurked in urban areas and preyed on the vulnerable. Before 1850 no laws governed the treatment of emigrants, either, so even legitimate business owners were free to take advantage of the general ignorance and confusion to make a profit.

Upon their arrival in Hamburg, tired and befuddled travelers were assailed by *Litzer* (runners) who had been hired by innkeepers, shipping companies, money exchangers, and others to bring in customers. *Litzer* were paid a commission for every customer they brought in and thus behaved, in the words of one man, "like so many pirates." [24] Many snatched luggage so that travelers had no choice but to follow them to a destination. Once in the clutches of unscrupulous businessmen, families often paid too much for food and lodging and bought goods that they did not need for the voyage.

In order to stop what some called "the runner's racket," a private group in Hamburg formed the Association for the Protection of Emigrants in about 1850. Members set up an information office near the train station so new arrivals could quickly get information on the average price of room and board as well as information on baggage transfer, rates of money exchange, and the different types of passage available to America.

Protection at Bremerhaven

Hamburg played a significant role in emigration, but it was secondary to Bremerhaven, the main port of embarkation for German emigrants in the late 1800s. Located about thirty miles from the mouth of the Weser River on the North Sea, the city of Bremen had been a seaport for centuries. By about 1825, however, the Weser

"A Pretty Good Trip"

In early 1865 Heinrich Moller boarded the steamship Teutonia *and began his voyage to America. After getting settled in Cumberland, Maryland, he wrote to his family, describing onboard conditions that would have made many immigrants envious. His account can be found in* News from the Land of Freedom: German Immigrants Write Home, *edited by Walter D. Kamphoefner, Wolfgang Helbich, and Ulrike Sommer.*

I will tell you what it was like on the ship. In the morning there was coffee and white bread, for lunch soup and different kinds of meat, bread, sometimes potatoes, plums, and dumplings. We made potato salad from the potatoes, . . . you could have as much vinegar, pepper and salt as you wanted. We had to go to get our own food like this, one after the other. There were 12 men together, there were 4 beds, in each bed there were 3 men. They went to get the food 2 by 2. In the evening there was tea. My bed was like this, in Hamburg [my friend] David and I bought 2 sacks of straw and covers. So I had 1 sack of straw and 2 covers, that was like a bed. Dear parents, brother, and sisters, the ocean crossings aren't as easy as one thinks, but I had a pretty good trip, thank God.

had become so filled with silt that many large ships were no longer able to reach the city's docks. Determined to solve the problem, city officials purchased land near the mouth of the river and built a new port, which they named Bremerhaven ("Bremen's Harbor"). The port received its first ship in 1830.

Bremen was the first city in Germany to offer aid and protection to emigrants.

A contemporary woodcut depicts the tourist, salon, and steerage class options available to immigrants sailing to America.

In addition to providing travel information and restricting the activities of *Litzer*, city officials sponsored the establishment of river barges to carry passengers downriver to Bremerhaven. In 1862 a rail connection was completed between the two, shortening the transfer time to just a few hours. The establishment of the first hotel for emigrants, the Auswandererhaus, in Bremerhaven gave travelers a place to rest, eat, and bathe before boarding their ship. The Auswandererhaus was so popular and so successful that it served as a model for others like it throughout Europe.

In their effort to protect emigrants, Bremen officials also regulated conditions aboard ships leaving Bremerhaven. In 1832 they passed laws requiring each ship to be seaworthy, provide space for each passenger to lie down, and have adequate food and water on board for ninety days at sea. In the past, shiploads of emigrants had starved, suffered, and died due to a lack of such basics. Each ship was also required to have regularly inspected toilet and washing facilities, and a doctor was to be on board for each voyage. Passenger acts passed by the United States in 1819 and 1855 also reinforced these standards.

Below Deck

In addition to the many complications they encountered in port cities, emigrants sometimes had to wait days or even weeks to board a ship. There were numerous reasons for the delays. Sometimes paperwork was incomplete. Sometimes repairs needed to be made before a ship could leave. Often there was no ship in port. Carl Berthold wrote in 1852, "We have been lying here [at Bremerhaven] for a week waiting for our ship that isn't here yet. Our ship, called the Liverpohl, is said to be lying in front of the canal and because of unfavorable winds cannot come in here, so we may be lying here several more days before we can get away." [25]

Once the ship was ready, however, steerage passengers were given a quick medical examination, were disinfected in an effort to keep fleas and lice in check, and were given a smallpox vaccination. Finally, they were allowed to board. As first- and second-class passengers made their way to roomy cabins, thousands of the poor were directed down steep stairways into steerage. Strict division between upper and lower levels allowed the wealthy to enjoy the crossing without ever coming in contact with those who were packed in the depths of the ship below.

The first glimpse of steerage—the crude space between the upper deck and the cargo hold—usually filled everyone with dismay and disbelief. Despite regulations, shipping lines spent very little on third-class facilities, so the low-ceilinged area was unfurnished except for rows of wooden berths that were nailed, one above the other, down the sides of the ship. Flooring was so flimsy that bilge water could be seen below. Rats sometimes scurried about. What little ventilation there was came from open hatches, and hanging oil lamps provided smoky light in the gloom. Passengers were expected to claim a berth and pack themselves, their families, and their bundles and bags into

a space that might be little more than six feet long and two feet high.

A few days at sea made conditions even worse. Seawater occasionally splashed into the open hatches, drenching mattresses and bedding. The rolling motion of the ship made many passengers seasick. Toilet facilities were usually inadequate, so many passengers used chamber pots, which sloshed and spilled when the ship bucked the waves. The smell of cargo in the hold—everything from fish to animal hides—mixed with other odors to create an overpowering smell. In 1911 a report from the U.S. Immigration Commission said of steerage:

> The unattended vomit of the seasick, the odors of not too clean bodies, the reek of food and the awful stench of the nearby toilet rooms make the atmosphere of the steerage such that it is a marvel that human flesh can endure it. . . . Most immigrants lie in their berths for most of the voyage, in a stupor caused by the foul air. The food often repels them. . . . It is almost impossible to keep personally clean. All of these conditions are naturally aggravated by the crowding. [26]

Poor Food, Foul Water

Even those who had an appetite complained about shipboard food, which shipping company advertisements sometimes described in glowing terms. One advertisement read:

> The passengers from the day of embarkation to the day of disembarkation

Steerage passengers like these often spent hours on deck in an effort to escape the cramped, unsanitary living quarters below.

at the port of destination receive free board. . . . This consists of sustaining and nutritious food such as salt beef, salt pork, herrings, peas, beans, pearl barley, oats, rice, sauerkraut, butter, plums, pastries, pudding, etc., all in sufficient quantity and of the best quality. Coffee is served in the mornings, and in the evenings tea and ship's bread with butter. In accordance with the decree of the local authority, the ships are provisioned for 90 days so that the passengers will not lack for anything on the longest voyage. [27]

Despite promises, food on board was generally inferior, especially in the early days of immigration. Everything was doled out in small amounts to ensure that the supplies that had been purchased would last until the voyage was over. No preservation methods were used, so bread became moldy by the end of the voyage, butter and pork fat rancid, and flour full of weevils.

Water, also advertised as being plentiful and fresh, was rationed, too, with a small amount set aside for each passenger for washing, cooking, and drinking. Even that quota could be foul tasting after being stored in casks that had previously held oil, vinegar, or turpentine. Immigrant William Bell remembered, "When it [the water] was drawn out of the casks, it was no clearer than that of a dirty kennel after a heavy shower of rain, so that its appearance alone was sufficient to sicken one. But its dirty appearance was not its worst quality. It had such a rancid smell, that, to be in the same neighbourhood, was enough to turn one's stomach." [28]

Batten the Hatches

Under the best conditions, ocean travel was uncomfortable for steerage passengers. Storms turned the crossing into a nightmare. When rain, wind, and waves lashed the decks, the hatches were battened down (secured) tightly, leaving no source of ventilation, except for a few pinhole or strainer-size holes, that were in the cover. The pitching of the ship increased the danger of fires, so lamps had to be put out and meals could not be prepared. Even the strongest passengers became ill, and injuries complicated matters. The turmoil was described by passenger Edwin Bottomley, who remembered:

Soon after we got to bed the ship began to roll very hard and the sea and wind began to roar as if it was bent on the destruction of everything floating upon it. . . . The luggage belonging to the passengers rolled about and cans and pots were strewed about in all places and the noise all made was beyond description. There was screaming and praying in every corner and the sailors cursing and the waves rolling all over the deck all at one time. [29]

German American photographer Alfred Stieglitz captured the crowded conditions immigrants endured aboard a transatlantic steamer in this 1907 photo.

Lifeboats and life preservers were not common at the time, so when ships went down in the worst storms, everyone on board was lost. Only if a ship was close to shore could passengers be rescued.

Storms were not the only life-threatening events that passengers faced, however. Diseases such as typhus and cholera were deadly as well. Typhus, carried by lice, was known as "ship fever" because it was so common. Cholera, an infection of the stomach and intestines, spread quickly once it struck. There were no cures for such afflictions, and despite regulations, there was often no doctor on board. Thus, passengers were left to take care of themselves, or they turned to the ship's captain, who had some crude medical experience and a medicine chest stocked with "remedies." These could include cream of tartar, peppermint extract, powdered rhubarb, or pills advertised as useful for curing a number of ailments.

Because disease was common and medical care inadequate, the death rate aboard a ship could be high, up to 10 percent in many cases. The elderly were most susceptible, as were infants and new mothers. There were times, however, when children were left orphaned when both their parents died, and sometimes entire families died and were buried at sea.

Even without problems brought on by storms or contagious diseases, an incompetent captain and crew could lead to widespread misery. Most seamen had the best interests of everyone at heart and made every effort to keep order and ensure that food and water were distributed fairly. Other crews, however, were care-less, irresponsible, and even cruel. They might withhold food and water or distribute them arbitrarily. They might ignore reports of lawbreaking, leaving passengers vulnerable to harassment, robbery, and assaults. On at least one ship, crews allowed the bodies of the dead to remain on board for days before burying them at sea. On another ship, rules were so strict that a passenger was handcuffed simply for using insulting language.

Some of the most corrupt crews even used bribery and coercion on the passengers. Single women who had no husband or male relative to protect them were the most vulnerable because they could be pressured for sexual favors in exchange for better treatment. As British consul William Mure reported, "[At least one captain] conducted himself harshly and in a most improper manner to some of the female passengers having held out the inducement of better rations to two who were almost starving in the hope they would accede [give in] to his infamous designs." [30]

Steamship Era

Beginning in the 1850s, steamships began to make the trip between Europe and America. After that, a direct voyage between Hamburg or Bremerhaven and New York, which had lasted between 40 and 65 days in previous years, was shortened to a maximum of two weeks.

The appearance of new ships meant that accommodations improved as well. Cooks were hired to take over kitchen chores, and menus expanded to include oatmeal, rice, molasses, sugar, and tea. For the sake of comfort and modesty, steerage was divided into sections so that single men slept forward in the ship, families amidship, and single women toward the rear. Wooden tables and benches were provided. Bathroom facilities were slightly improved, although they were usually located on an upper deck and were still inadequate for large numbers of people.

Although steamships were vastly better than earlier vessels, the U.S. Immigration Commission still found conditions to be too cramped and public to be ideal. It wrote in 1911:

> Imagine a large room, perhaps seven feet in height, extending the entire breadth of the ship and about one-third of its length. . . . This room is filled with a framework of iron pipes, forming a double tier of six-by-two-feet berths, with only sufficient space left to serve as aisles or passageways. . . . Such a compartment will sometimes accommodate as many as three hundred passengers and is duplicated in other parts of the ship and on other decks. [31]

Anxiety and Anticipation

Even under these less-than-perfect conditions, passengers learned to manage and make do. To escape the confines of steerage, for instance, many went out on the steerage deck, where they walked or sat for hours at a time. Philip Taylor writes, "Day after day . . . passengers heard the creaking of timbers, the shouts of sailors, the wash of water against the hull." [32] Men smoked and played cards. Women sewed and talked. Some speculated about what their new lives would be like in America. Some practiced speaking English. Others rehearsed answering questions they would be asked in immigration stations when they landed. At times, musicians entertained with their songs, and everyone enjoyed moments of excitement when a ship, whales, or distant icebergs were sighted.

By the time the voyage was over, however, those immigrants who had survived the rigors of the Atlantic were more than ready to be back on solid ground. The sight of land filled them with joy. With tears in their eyes, they gathered up their children and their belongings and waited for the moment when they would be allowed ashore.

In the midst of their anticipation, however, anxiety nagged. The next stage of their journey was immediately before them. There was no knowing if life in their new homeland would be good or bad. They could only wait for the days ahead to reveal the further challenges and adventures that were in store.

CHAPTER THREE

All Ashore!

Most German newcomers were eager to begin life in America. They were prepared to work hard and triumph over numerous obstacles as they adapted to a new world.

Some of those obstacles would include port officials and red tape, swindlers and con men, and overland journeys to distant locales. As their ship drew into port, however, all that everyone could think about was the waterfront that lay directly ahead. Martin Weitz, who arrived in New York City in 1854, remembered his feelings: "On the 17th of June in the morning we saw land, . . . at 12 o'clock midday we arrived in the harbor. I had never seen anything like it, it's like you were looking at a forest (of masts), then it was joy upon

joy, you can imagine that, now we're getting somewhere."[33]

After 1886 the Statue of Liberty added to everyone's excitement as they entered New York's harbor. The 151-foot figure, a gift from France to the United States, seemed like an overwhelming preview of coming attractions. One German, who was nearing his eightieth birthday, described the statue's impact on him: "I thought she was one of the seven wonders of the world."[34]

Ports of Entry
Most immigrants entered the United States by way of the New York harbor, but there were other ports throughout the country where thousands went ashore.

Those who had relatives or friends who had settled in states like Missouri, Texas, or California, for instance, usually landed as near to them as possible. Immigration expert Ira Glazier states, "People went places where they had relatives or townspeople. There wasn't a great deal of choice. Destinations were determined by the network, by the chain." [35]

There were many reasons for entering the country in ports other than New York, however. New Orleans welcomed a great number of German immigrants because fares to that city were cheaper. Those who wanted to travel west often preferred Baltimore. This was because the North German Lloyd Steamship Line established an agreement with the Baltimore and Ohio Railroad in 1867, so that immigrants could buy and use a single ticket for the crossing to Baltimore and a trip farther west by train. The pier in Baltimore's harbor was even constructed so that immigrants could proceed directly to waiting trains. Because of its connections and services, Baltimore became second only to New York in the number of immigrants it received.

Some immigrants landed in Quebec, Canada, because they could more easily travel by water down the St. Lawrence River and across the Great Lakes to northern states like Michigan and Minnesota. The city offered helpful information to newcomers, including a handbook that encouraged them to make Canada their final home. One paragraph read:

Many have regretted when too late that they did not . . . take advantage of

For immigrants entering New York harbor after 1886, the Statue of Liberty was a welcome sight after their long voyage.

the frequent opportunities that presented themselves for settlement in convenient situations in Upper or Lower Canada, instead of squandering their means and valuable time to looking after an imaginary Paradise in the aguish [fever-producing] swamps of Illinois and Missouri, or other distant regions of the Western States. [36]

Castle Garden

Because immigrants were relatively few in number and seemed to present little threat to other Americans before 1850, even New York City officials paid little attention to them before that time. A doctor usually rowed out from a quarantine office located on Staten Island to meet each ship and ensure that it was free of contagious diseases such as smallpox. The ill were rejected— sent back to Germany on the next ship—or quarantined until they were well. Those who were healthy went ashore and made their way into the city and beyond as best they could. For those who came from small villages, entering the city was often overwhelming. Anna Klinger wrote in 1849, "The city of New York is the largest in America, it is so big you can't walk around it in one day. . . . Here you can find people from all corners of the world, there are about 4,000 German residents alone." [37]

Beginning in 1855, newcomers to New York began stepping off their ship onto a barge that took them to Castle Garden, a station specifically set up to receive and process immigrants. Located on the southern tip of Manhattan Island, Castle Garden was originally Castle Clinton, a federal fort built in 1811 to guard the city and harbor from possible British invasion. Between 1823 and 1854 the fort was converted into a restaurant, entertainment center, opera house, and theater. In 1855 it became an immigrant landing depot. Between that year and 1890, when Ellis Island became the official entry spot for immigrants, more than 8 million people entered the United States through the Castle's doors.

Disembarking at Castle Garden was usually a scene of confusion. Officials shouted orders in a variety of languages. Eager crowds jostled each other. Families,

Immigrants arriving in New York were processed at Castle Garden until 1890, when Ellis Island (pictured) became the city's official immigration station.

the ground still swaying under their feet, got separated in the commotion. Baggage was lugged away and sometimes lost. One new arrival remembered:

> The emigrants proceed in a body up the corridor into the interior of the building, their boxes and baggage being removed to the luggage warehouses, and here they range themselves . . . on the seats. In front of them, and in the centre of the building, which is lit by a glass dome, stand a staff of some dozen gentlemen, all busily engaged in making arrangements for facilitating the movements and promoting the settlement of the newly-arrived emigrants. [38]

Everyone eventually made their way into lines and waited for registration and a medical inspection. Passengers were checked for contagious disease—cholera, plague, smallpox, typhoid fever, yellow fever, scarlet fever, measles, and diphtheria—as well as for mental illness and trachoma, an eye disease that caused blindness and even death. The latter was the reason for more than half of all medical detentions, and its discovery meant certain deportation back to Germany.

Due to the large numbers of people, the wait at Castle Garden generally took hours. After immigrants were processed, however, they could leave or take advantage of some of the other amenities offered at the depot. These included a money exchange, where rates were updated three times a day and were prominently displayed. Newcomers could also buy railroad tickets, send telegrams, deposit their valuables for a short time, and wait for friends who were coming to meet them. One observer wrote in 1856 that new arrivals could also "enjoy themselves in the depot by taking their meals, cleansing themselves in the spacious bath-rooms, or promenading on the galleries or on the dock." [39]

Aid and Advice

Solicitors could not enter Castle Garden, but unscrupulous individuals were always waiting outside the immigration depot. Pickpockets and street thieves snatched valuables. Cab drivers overcharged their fares. Runners and agents who worked for railroads, steamboats, and boardinghouses pressured and bullied anyone they could into accompanying them to their destination.

Perhaps the most devious individuals were former immigrants who posed as helpful passersby. After gaining the newcomers' trust, they then stole from them or conned them out of their money. Angela Heck remembered the situation she and her fellow passengers stumbled into in New York City in 1854:

> There was a young man there from Hefnig near Echternach who was there to meet his countrymen, a real rascal. Then he led all of us who were in the ship to a German boardinghouse in New York. There we ate three meals and slept one night. Then everyone had to pay 7 francs (about $1.40). My husband had to pay 14 francs for the two of us, since they had put all the trunks in the cellar and

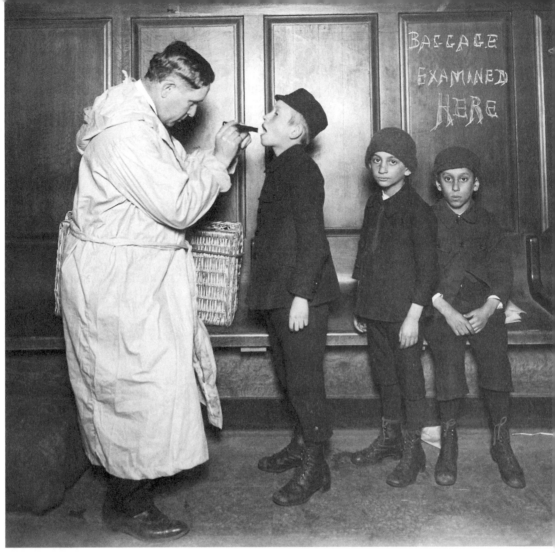

Once they arrived in America, immigrants like these children were examined for signs of trachoma, smallpox, typhoid fever, and other diseases.

no one could get them back before he paid. . . . It was all very sad. Most of them didn't have enough money and couldn't go where they wanted. [40]

There were those who were genuinely helpful and generous with their time, knowledge, and resources, however. Journalist Henry Villard wrote of one such Good Samaritan when he arrived in New York in 1853:

My landing upon American soil took place under anything but auspicious circumstances. I was utterly destitute of money . . . and I literally did not know a single person in New York or elsewhere in the Eastern States to whom I could . . . apply for help and counsel. To crown all, I could not speak a word of English. A traveling companion who had tried to persuade me to accompany him to California noticed my depression, and guessed its cause. . . . He generously offered to lend me twenty dollars, which I accepted, of course, with joy. [41]

Reputable groups such as the German Society also did their best to help newcomers. Founded by caring German Americans who were already established in the United States, the organization aimed to provide money, clothing, and other necessaries of life to the poor in their communities. Noticing that new arrivals needed help, too, however, it established information bureaus in cities such as New York, Baltimore, Philadelphia, St. Louis, Cincinnati, and Chicago. According to author Philip Taylor, their agents also "met ships, warded off runners, helped secure food and shelter, and, on occasion, gave Germans small sums of money." [42]

Kleindeutschland

Once the confusion of the harbor was behind them, immigrants set about the next step of their journey—getting to a final destination where they could find shelter and a job. Many knew those who had immigrated before and were intent on joining up with them. Others had no waiting friends or family and thus looked for a community where they could feel secure, communicate with people, and find work.

The neighborhood known as Kleindeutschland ("Little Germany") met the requirements of those who wanted to settle in New York City. Kleindeutschland was located on Manhattan's lower east side where German immigrants had begun settling in the early 1800s. Characterized by brownstone tenement houses divided into businesses below and tiny apartments upstairs, it was home to about seventy-five thousand people, all of them German. New arrivals found it to be the nearest thing to Germany in the New World. Karl Theodor Griesinger wrote in 1863, "The resident of *Kleindeutschland* need not even know English in order to make a living, which is a considerable attraction to the immigrant." [43]

Thousands of newcomers flocked to Kleindeutschland, appreciating the fact that its butcher shops, bakeries, pharmacies, and doctors' offices were owned and patronized by Germans. The neighborhood had a German library, a school, and a large park, known as Weisse Garten ("White Garden"). There were many opportunities to find jobs in the neighborhood itself, and its closeness to New York's business district offered other possibilities for employment, too.

Living accommodations were available in the neighborhood, but most were extremely small apartments, usually little more than a ten-by-ten-foot living room and a bedroom. These were generally dark, airless, and smelled strongly of sauerkraut. Oftentimes, living rooms were used as workshops, so there was little space in which to move about. Immigrants were willing to put up with the poor conditions, however, because rents were low, sometimes only five or six dollars a month. Griesinger writes, "According to the standards of the German workingman, one can live like a prince for ten to fourteen dollars

Cramped and Dangerous

Although many German immigrants were willing to live in tenements until they improved their economic status, the conditions they endured there were not only overcrowded but also dangerous. Author Doris Weatherford details some of the hazards in her book Foreign and Female: Immigrant Women in America, 1840–1930.

Fire was a constant threat. Most tenements were old, wooden, and had only one exit. The fact that each apartment had its own stove multiplied the danger. . . . When fire escapes were required by building codes, the space-starved immigrant family extended itself into this available area. Periodic raids by the fire department could not permanently remove the washtubs, flowerpots, clotheslines, and extra chests packed into their escape way. Once a fire started, the proximity [closeness] of houses made them a death trap for hundreds. . . .

A second danger was epidemics, which spread as rapidly as fire. . . . Although public attention was drawn to the problem when an epidemic hit, few realized that . . . tenements were constant disease mills. It was a rare person who was not exposed to tuberculosis. A third of a million rooms in New York City were without windows. . . . One national health authority said of the rooms where [people] lived day in and day out, "If we had invented machines to create tuberculosis we could not have succeeded better."

German American families in overcrowded tenement housing lived in constant fear of fires and health epidemics.

a month. Apartments at this price contain two bedrooms, two living rooms, one of which is used for a kitchen, and sufficient room for storing coal and wood." [44]

Traveling Inland

While many immigrants stayed in New York City, others went on to other states with large German American populations, including Pennsylvania, Ohio, Wisconsin, Minnesota, and Illinois. Early Germans had settled in these northern states not only for the rich land and industrial opportunities but also because the South had a slave-based economy prior to 1861. Slavery was a strong reminder of the serf system their ancestors had struggled under in Germany, so most immigrants detested it. Martin Weitz was one of these, and he included his thoughts in a letter home in 1856: "Immigrants can do a lot and they will continue to work for the good cause [abolition of slavery] and those who wallow still in error they will wake up and say, Long live freedom. . . . Down with slavery." [45]

Travel inland was a lengthy and exhausting process for newcomers. In the early nineteenth century, most travelers had little choice but to go on foot, by wagon, or by stage, although water transportation quickly became a popular alternative, especially after the Erie Canal opened in 1825. Then travelers could go up the Hudson River and take the canal to Buffalo, New York. Many travelers then made their way from New York across Ohio to the Ohio River, where flatboats, keelboats, and the newer steamboats plied the waters. Some also used the Mississippi and Missouri Rivers to travel farther north and west.

Railroads that crisscrossed the nation after the Civil War allowed immigrants to travel with greater ease and speed to their destinations. Railroad companies even offered free land as an incentive for immigrants to buy tickets. Travel by rail was challenging, however, especially at the beginning of the journey when immigrants were the most confused and vulnerable. Train stations were usually large and busy, and signs and announcements were printed in English, which no one could read. Travelers often bought expensive tickets to wrong destinations and paid for services that were free, such as the transfer of baggage. After a long wait in the ticket line, they usually had to go from train to train until they found the correct one. Once aboard, they sat for hours on uncomfortable wooden benches, propped against their bags and bundles, and stretching their legs only when they rushed out to buy food at a stop.

The numerous connections that had to be made to get to a destination cost money, and most immigrants were unprepared for this expense, too. Heinrich Moller remembered that he spent his last few dollars to purchase a ticket for a journey from New York to Cumberland, Maryland, unaware that the ticket got him only as far as Harrisburg, Pennsylvania. He was forced to ask a stranger to give him seventy-five cents, which allowed him to get as far as Baltimore. There, he was stranded, penniless and depressed. He remembered:

The Erie Canal

A final leg of an immigrant's journey was often accomplished by boat on the Erie Canal, a man-made waterway that links Albany and Buffalo, New York. In The Germans in America, 1607–1970, *edited by Howard B. Furer, immigrant Jacob Schramm gives his impressions of travel on the canal.*

We arranged for the trip to Buffalo in a canalboat: sleeping quarters and meals with the captain, 8 dollars each. This is a distance of 360 English miles . . . and the trip lasted 7 days. . . . The boats are not very large, about 50 feet long and 10 wide, with the lower deck just high enough so a man can stand upright; nevertheless everything is surprisingly well managed. People of this region, therefore, make constant use of these boats, and it never occurs to anyone to go by foot, to ride, or travel by carriage. . . .

The boat is drawn by horses [walking on each side of the canal], usually in relays of two, and day and night they keep up a sharp pace. The canal is only 4 or 5 feet deep, and of course the boats are built in accordance. For the most part they are the property of companies in New York or Albany. . . . There are also people who use the canals independently, but they cannot take passengers, because they have to have their own horses with them all the way. When one pair is tired, they are brought aboard and fed while the other team is hitched to the boat, and so they alternate. Every boat has to have a man to drive the horses. The companies that have so many boats have farms at different stations, where they keep a large number of horses, and where the horses are changed and fresh drivers provided.

When I got to Baltimore there was no friends and no one I knew, I stood there all alone like I was lost. Then, all of a sudden I remembered [a former countryman] Ernzt Traudmann. . . . I searched for 3 hours before I found him. I told him that I didn't have any money and wanted to go to Lottig's in Cumberland. . . . Traudmann bought me the ticket, that cost another 4 1/2 dollars, it cost 1 dollar to bring my trunk from the train station to Traudmann's and from Traudmann's back to the other train station another 2 1/2 dollars. [46]

Milwaukee and Cincinnati

Wisconsin was a popular destination for immigrants, although it often took ten days to get there. Despite the long journey, the state had many attractions for German newcomers. Its farmland was rich. It offered liberal voting rights to immigrants. The presence of a Catholic bishop in Milwaukee appealed to many German Catholics.

Milwaukee was known as the German Athens because of its large German population and many cultural opportunities. As one traveler to the city stated in the 1850s, there were "German houses, German inscriptions over the doors or on signs, and German faces everywhere. . . . Many Germans who live here learn no English and they seldom exit from their own German section of the city."[47] In the city, most newcomers could find work in small businesses already owned by Germans, or they could rent or buy land outside of town and start farming. By 1890 Wisconsin was known as the most Germanic state in the United States due to the large influx of immigrants in midcentury.

While thousands of German immigrants went to Milwaukee, thousands more made their way to Cincinnati, Ohio, another urban center that was known for its large German population. By 1870 almost fifty thousand immigrant families resided in the Over-the-Rhine section of town, so-called because crossing the Miami and Erie Canal, which bordered the neighborhood, was like crossing the Rhine River into Germany.

Like Kleindeutschland, Over-the-Rhine was wholly German in character. It had a variety of industries, including lumberyards, foundries, pork packers, tanneries, and breweries. There were shops—bakeries, butcher shops, shoemakers, and department stores. For entertainment, there were numerous theaters and opera houses and the grand Music Hall, or *Saenger-*

In this late-nineteenth-century illustration, German immigrants lost in New York ask a gentleman for directions.

halle, built for the first Cincinnati music festival that took place in May 1873. At the conclusion of the festival the *Chicago Tribune* labeled Cincinnati "the first musical city of the West." [48]

Newcomers to Over-the-Rhine usually crowded their families into tiny apartments, often located above businesses. Everyone dreamed, however, of the time when they could buy a home, and the establishment of several building-and-loan associations (*Bauervereine*) made that dream a reality for many. A family only had to contribute twenty-five to fifty cents per week; then, when a significant sum had been collected, members drew straws to see who could purchase property and build a home. The *Bauervereine* eventually evolved into the main lending institutions of Cincinnati. Author Daniel W. Young writes:

They were, for the most part, localized institutions with such names as Green Street #2 Loan and Building Company and 11th Ward Building Association #2. Others were more widespread and had such names as Germania Building Association #2, Teutonia Loan and Building Company, Central Turner Building Association, German Building Association #7, and others. [49]

A Good Country

Despite the fact that most German immigrants made their homes in northern states, there were those who settled in southern regions. St. Louis, Missouri, was a popular destination because members of the Giessen Emigration Society (a society led by German radicals Friedrich Münch and Paul Follen, whose goal was to establish a "new Germany" in America) had settled there in the 1830s and 1840s. By 1860 German Americans made up the largest ethnic group in the city.

Some Germans settled in Texas as well, creating ethnic pockets in the north central, northern, and western parts of the state. In 1880 the population of San Antonio was one-third German. The city's first suburb, the well-to-do King William district, was settled in the late nineteenth century by prosperous German merchants, who named the twenty-five block area after Kaiser Wilhelm. Other residents of San Antonio had a less respectful nickname for the neighborhood, which lay on a curve of the San Antonio River. They called it "Sauerkraut Bend." [50]

No matter where immigrants settled—and some traveled all the way to California, Oregon, and Washington before they found a locale that suited their taste and temperament—they had to be resilient in order to survive. Many suffered hardship and disappointment, disillusionment and frustration. Nevertheless, most were convinced that good experiences would eventually outweigh the bad. As immigrant Johann Pritzlaff wrote, "America is a good country, it blossoms under God's blessing, but it bears thorns and thistles as well. For a man who works, it is much better here than over there." [51]

CHAPTER FOUR

Newcomers in a New World

A lthough newcomers had dreamed of America as a land of golden opportunities, everyone found that reality was extremely different. There were so many adjustments to be made. A person had to interact with strangers, work at a new job, find one's way around an unfamiliar neighborhood, and make oneself understood, all at the same time. Carl Berthold wrote, "You can easily imagine how things are when you first come to a foreign country and can't speak the language, how things are *at first* and how one feels." [52]

There was a bright side, however. The loneliness and stress were eased by the existence of German American communities and by the support of already established immigrants. The newcomers' willingness to work hard, adapt to American ways, and persevere in the face of discouragement also helped them as they faced the first months and years in the New World.

Coping with the Unexpected

Many immigrants suffered from acute homesickness and loneliness for a time after their arrival. Family members and friends were far away in Germany, probably never to be seen again. Even those who immigrated together sometimes went their separate ways. Because of the vast

German families like this one in New Mexico often banded together to help each other as they established homes and farms in the New World.

distances between cities or homesteads, they were often out of touch with each other. Making new friends was difficult for those who lived in rural areas where neighbors were miles away. Young single men, who might have found companionship through marriage, often waited several years to become financially secure before settling down with a wife.

Some immigrants encountered unexpected setbacks such as illness or injury that were serious roadblocks on the path to prosperity. Even a short period of unemployment sometimes forced immigrants to write to family members back in Germany, appealing for money. Some would have returned home if they could have afforded it. Ludwig Dilger, who underwent several operations in the course of one year, was one of these. He wrote

his parents in 1886, "I would have liked to come home a long time ago, but it's hard to get the money together and when you do, some illness comes along and takes away every hard-earned dollar." [53]

American customs and habits could be unexpectedly objectionable, too. Christian Kirst expressed his views: "The Americans don't live like the Germans, no one saves for the future, shoes, stockings, and clothing aren't mended. . . . Here the woman rules the roost. . . . The children of the poorer classes are very badly brought up." [54] Despite such critical observations, however, Kirst had to admit that America's advantages outweighed the drawbacks. "There's only one thing I regret that I spent so many years over there [in Germany], if I had come here 20 years ago then I'd probably be a rich man by now." [55]

Fitting In

Although they often did not fully understand American habits and customs, most German immigrants believed that the best way to get ahead was to fit in. Thus, many Americanized their names almost immediately, both to appear less foreign and to eliminate any difficulty that employers and others might have had with spelling and pronunciation. Thus, *Johann* would change to *John*, and *Heinrich* became *Henry*. A family with the last name *Klein*, might take its English equivalent—*Small*. *Braun* was changed to *Brown*, *Schmidt* to *Smith*, *Becker* to *Baker*.

Traditional German clothing branded an immigrant as foreign even more surely than a German name. Newcomers in odd-looking garments were made fun of and sometimes had trouble finding work. Thus, everyone usually packed embroidered skirts, shawls, knee-length pants, and distinctive hats away in trunks and purchased dresses, trousers, and hats similar to those worn by other working-class Americans.

Young people in particular sometimes spent a large percentage of their wages on clothing in order to fit in. One man wrote to his mother in Germany in 1852, "Dear mother, you ought to see me now with my new clothes, long black coat, black vest and trousers, choker, black silk hat, and my hair parted not only on the top but also on the back of the head! I suppose it looks funny, but then you must do as the Romans, or they will point at you: 'Look there, that Dutchman.'" [56]

The younger generation was also the most determined to learn to speak English as quickly as possible. Most young Germans practiced as often as possible and took pride in their new language skills. They cheerfully accepted the teasing they got for their mistakes and their broken accents, knowing that practice would soon smooth away any problems. Wilhelmine Wiebusch wrote of her experiences and those of her friend Anna Beckermann when they served as maids in an American household: "You should just hear us speaking English, we just rattle off what we hear, whether it's right or not, the Lady (Mrs. Silvia Moses) says sometimes she almost dies laughing at us." [57]

A German boy and girl pose in traditional dress. Most German immigrants shed their traditional garb as they tried to assimilate themselves.

Long Hours, Low Pay

Finding work was a top priority with Wiebusch and nearly every German immigrant when they reached America, especially after discovering that everything from food to farm equipment was more expensive than in Germany. In order to get ahead, everyone had to compromise, budget carefully, and even sacrifice. Wilhelm Stille wrote home in 1840, "You want to know how poor families here get along, they rent a room or a chamber and then they work for a daily wage in the rain, snow, and cold wind and when such people are lucky, in 4 to 6 years they can maybe earn enough to buy a 40 acre piece of bush. . . . A weak man can't get through it." [58]

Getting a job was sometimes harder than expected, especially if one's arrival coincided with a national or regional slump in the economy. Martin Weitz, who arrived during a recession in the 1850s, remembered:

I looked around for work in New York and the area, but all for nothing. . . . Thousands and thousands were wandering around without work, without money, without food, dying of hunger. . . . They poured through the town in great droves demanding that work be found for them, but all for nothing. All over America it was terrible. . . . prices went way up and still are. [59]

If an immigrant had a skill, he or she sometimes found work with another German artisan who had already established a business. Generally, every newcomer had to be satisfied with an entry-level position, however. "When I arrived in Chicago . . . I was lucky enough to find employment right that afternoon, & although the conditions were not brilliant, I accepted, because I had nothing better in sight for the moment," [60] wrote Johann Bauer in 1855. Hours were generally long and pay was low, but the hope of advancement or a better job helped many immigrants persevere.

Even those who were lucky enough to find work in their chosen field were sometimes disappointed. "It's not quite like what we'd imagined," wrote Mathias Dorgathen, who had been a miner in Germany. "Work is scarce at the mines here, . . . [and] the wages aren't as high as the others always wrote." [61]

Women's Work

With a need for money, female immigrants often went out to work, too, despite the fact that in Germany most had devoted their lives to children and household chores. Young unmarried women were among the first to enter the workplace, finding employment as bakers, laundresses, nurses, and shop workers. Some went to work in factories, although only the strongest could remain there for any length of time. A U.S. Senate investigation in 1909 revealed the grueling conditions at a nut-and-bolt-making plant:

Much of the work is singularly [especially] unpleasant in character. . . . The action of the machine spatters oil or water over everything . . . including the operator and her clothing. . . . A woman . . . turning out the maximum number of

The Role of German Women

Even though German women worked outside the home upon their arrival in America, they continued to shoulder more traditional responsibilities, too. Author Richard H. Zeitlin describes their duties in an article, "Germans in Wisconsin," found on the Internet at http://home.dwave.net/~dhuehner/germanwis.html.

The role of the German woman throughout the pioneer era cannot be overestimated. In addition to bearing and caring for children, women had constantly to prepare meals without the benefit of many basic necessities. Tending the garden, the major source of the family's food supply, took much of the woman's time, in addition to which [if she lived on a farm and did not work outside the home] she was expected to work in the wheat or corn fields alongside the men, for the European practice of women working in the field was a cultural transfer from the Old Country. "Back to work again accompanied by the good mother . . . to aid us in the fields . . . until after sundown . . . " [immigrant farmer Johann Diederichs wrote]. In fact, everything involved women's labor, unless the task proved to be beyond their strength.

one-fourth inch nuts must press the treadle 50 times a minute—a rate which, in view of the fact that it is to be kept up for 60 minutes an hour and 10 hours a day, needs no comment. [62]

Although such work exhausted all who took it on, most did not complain because even the low wages they earned were higher than they could have made in Germany.

One type of job that was particularly popular with immigrant women was that of domestic servant. The polite attitudes of young Germans who had been trained by their parents to have a respect for authority and for their social superiors, made them popular with their American employers, too.

Servants were daily exposed to American lifestyles and thus were quickly able to understand and assimilate every aspect of American culture. They learned how Americans interacted, entertained, decorated their homes, and treated their children. If employers were rich, their servants worked in a beautiful setting, had their own bedroom, plenty to eat, and clean uniforms to wear. Many were even given the employers' cast-off clothing, which could be of high quality. One letter, written by immigrant Emilie Koenig in 1853, noted of maids in Lafayette, Indiana, "They are dressed like the grandest ladies when they come to church. . . . They really behave like genteel ladies." [63]

The biggest advantage was wages. Whereas a servant in Germany might earn only $8.25 a year, in New York she could earn almost twice that amount each month. Work hours were still long—a maid got up before dawn to light fires and make breakfast and usually was the last one to go to bed. Housework was unending due to the lack of laborsaving devices. Still, the benefits more than made up for the hardships.

Life on the Plains

While many immigrants coped with the challenges and complications of city life, those who had come to America to farm faced obstacles as well. America's "free land" was not exactly what they had been led to believe in Germany. Land around market towns was often already owned, and if it was for sale, it cost too much. Families who wanted to buy land had to spend several months or years working and saving just to be able to afford a small farm or a plot of unimproved woodland. Thus, the majority chose to move farther west, settling on the plains where land was cheap, rich, and plentiful.

Living on the plains was less expensive, but it was also a hard, lonely life. Friends and family were miles away. There were no churches or schools nearby. If a person got sick, a doctor was usually too far away to give medical care.

Preparing the land for farming—especially clearing brush and cutting down trees—was grueling labor. Few could afford to buy farm equipment, teams of horses, seeds, and supplies all at once. Christian Lenz wrote, "I bought myself a horse . . . now I still don't have a wagon or a plow or any seed and no harness for the horse and all the other things I need." [64] Most had to borrow money in order to get the goods they needed immediately.

On a new homestead, housing was a top priority, but with little money a family's first home had to be small—often no more than a twelve-by-twelve-foot room. Settlers were not always skilled carpenters, so the house was usually crudely constructed. Doors and windows (if there were any) let in the heat and cold. Roofs leaked. Chimneys smoked. Families had no choice but to eat and sleep in these tiny shacks, however, often sharing one bed. Some even brought farm animals indoors when they needed protection from freezing outdoor temperatures in the winter.

Those immigrants who had trees on their land and could build wooden homes felt luckier than families who settled where there were no trees. The latter, however, used their ingenuity to cut blocks of sod—soil held together by thick, matted roots—out of the prairie itself. These were then piled one on top of the other to build walls. Roofs were thatched and could be covered with sod as well.

Such houses had their advantages— they were fireproof, cool in summer, and warm in winter. They were damp, however, and inclined to settle and become lopsided. They were also home to snakes and small animals that burrowed into them for shelter. Bertha Frahm recalls her grandparents' sod home in Nebraska: "Mother used to tell of how snakes came in and drank milk from the crocks on the shelves, and how it rained in. They'd try to keep the bedding dry by covering it with oil-cloth [water-resistant fabric]." [65]

Patience and Common Sense

Although no immigrant family had much land at first, they made the most of what they had and relied on patience, common sense, and sound farming practices to gradually gain ground. They carefully rotated crops and made liberal use of fertilizer to guard the richness of the soil. They carefully cared for their livestock, constructing barns as soon as they could rather than leaving animals in the fields during cold weather as some American farmers did.

Many increased their chances of success by growing crops that were in high demand in America. In states like Ohio, Indiana, Illinois, Missouri, and Iowa, they focused on planting corn, a crop that was seldom grown in Germany. An immigrant in Missouri wrote home in 1861, "Corn . . . that's the most important thing in America, man and beast live from it." [66] Many Germans who emigrated from Russia also concentrated on wheat farming after they discovered that conditions for growing it were ideal in Kansas and other prairie states.

After a few years, many settlers had made visible progress. For instance, Johann Bauer began as a farmhand in 1860 and owned a farm worth three thousand dollars by the 1870s. He wrote in 1867:

A pioneer family poses with their donkey in front of their sod house. Unable to afford land elsewhere, many German Americans settled on the plains.

First Things First

When immigrants could not afford to buy large, well-established homesteads, they made creative compromises, renting or buying uncleared land, bartering for goods, and relying on neighbors for free labor. In an article found on the Internet at http://home.dwave.net/~dhuehner/germanwis.html, *author Richard H. Zeitlin describes how many immigrants built a home and settled in soon after their arrival.*

Building a house took about four weeks, often with the assistance of neighbors. In this early stage, bartering took the place of cash. Logs were common items of trade, and in one case a hundred feet of logs could be traded for fifty feet of boards.

Farm produce was also a common medium of exchange. Having secured a roof over his family's heads, the German immigrant turned his full attention to felling trees and clearing enough land for a subsistence garden and later for the larger scale farming which would enable him to enter the cash economy as soon as possible. Most of these initial "farms" were hardly more than large gardens. In the words of one German farmer, "The earth between the stumps is freed from roots as far as practicable, the earth tilled, and the potatoes are inserted." Johann Diederichs described the state of his farm as it was in 1849: "I now have cleared two acres, part of which I intend to use as a garden and on part of which I shall plant potatoes, corn, and beans."

When I first started to make my home on this great prairie, conditions were such that it would have caused great expense to build myself a good house and since I didn't have the means to carry out such a project, I decided to build myself a small temporary house, intending to build a better one as soon as my circumstances would allow. The time has now come. [67]

Despite their more comfortable circumstances, Bauer and others remained frugal even as they expanded their farms and enlarged and upgraded their homes.

Old and New Traditions

Hard work and thrift were important qualities to struggling German immigrants, but they took time for other activities, too. Family and church were extremely important. Earlier immigrants had established many Protestant and Catholic churches in their neighborhoods, so, in urban areas at least, newcomers found plenty of places to worship. Weddings and funerals provided distractions from the daily grind. The fact that old traditions were sometimes modified to suit the New World was exciting as well. For instance, bridal parties in Germany commonly wore black at their celebrations, but Herman Holle's bride chose to be different. Margarethe Winkelmeier (a wedding guest) shared the news with her parents: "The bridegroom had three boys on his side and the bride three girls. These girls were all dressed in snowy white, they looked wonderful all standing there." [68]

Immigrants who settled in German neighborhoods were able to enjoy traditional German holidays such as Fastnacht—a street carnival that took place the evening before Lent. They also looked forward to bock beer celebrations after Easter. Bock beer was darker and had a higher alcohol content than ordinary beer and was produced for a very short period of time each year. Traditional American holidays, especially Thanksgiving and Independence Day, were observed as well. Johann Bauer wrote to his parents on the Fourth of July, "Wherever there is a settlement, some kind of celebration will take place. We too, here on our quiet farm, will all get together and celebrate the holiday, no doubt with some fried chicken and other good things." [69]

Germans generally celebrated all their holidays with food, and in their letters home, immigrants often boasted about the amount and variety of good things to eat in America. Christian Kirst observed, "I get a poor wage but live like on holidays over there, we have meat and vegetables for lunch every day; bread here is like cake." [70] Many happily reported that they were putting on weight, a sign that they were comfortably well off. "There is certainly no burgher [comfortable middle-class citizen] in [the town of] Lengerich who eats or drinks better than I, here it's nothing special if you have ham and roasts

3 times a day, since that's normal," [71] wrote Ernst Stille.

Although most adapted to American foods and recipes as quickly as possible, eventually immigrants began cooking dishes that they had loved in the old country, too. Favorites included blood sausage, smoked goose, and a stew made of goose and duck wings, livers, gizzards, and hearts cooked with apples and dumplings. Schnitzel (veal cutlet) and sauerkraut were also widely enjoyed.

Societies and Clubs

Music was a significant part of German immigrant life, and newcomers often took part in musical groups that had been established by earlier immigrants. Singing societies were popular, particularly because they were virtually free. Attendance was also high at oratorios, light operas,

Ludwig van Beethoven's symphonies were frequently performed in German American concert halls.

and symphonies featuring the music of renowned German composers Beethoven, Bach, Handel, and others. Musical productions were usually performed in opera houses or music halls that had been constructed by the German community itself.

One particularly popular musical event was the Saengerfest, or "Singing Festival," wherein singing societies from around the region came together for days of pageantry, singing, and competitions. The fests were widely advertised. A parade might herald opening night, and performances took place in a large hall and included children's choirs, combined choirs from several societies, renowned soloists, and famous choir leaders. A grand banquet usually took place afterward, followed by a ball. Orchestras and bands from far and wide accompanied the various events.

German immigrants loved to be part of clubs and social organizations, too. Carl Entenmann told the Historical Association of Los Angeles in 1929, "We have a say-

The Wild West

While most immigrants settled in the East and the Midwest, a few went farther west, looking for riches or adventure. In News from the Land of Freedom, *immigrant Carl Blumner, one of the few Germans who settled in New Mexico, writes to his mother about his brother August's death in California and his own successful life in Santa Fe in 1852.*

August came here, to Santa Fe, in the spring of 1849; but he only stayed with me for a few months, and went from here to California, thinking and hoping to make a fortune more quickly there. He arrived safely in California. . . . I finally received a letter the following year from his brother-in-law, who informed me that he had died in August 1850 in the gold mines on the Yuba River, in California. He fell ill with abdominal ailments, and he passed away, calm and composed, after about a month. . . .

I've been married about 4 years; my wife is a Mexican, the youngest daughter of a good but poor family. . . . My business here has almost always been as a merchant; about a year ago I gave up my trading company and am mostly employed in the service of the government. Since the United States took possession of this country . . . since the year 1846, I have always had one or the other government post; *Treasurer (Schatzmeister), Collector (Erster Steuereinnehmer), Vice Secretair* (the second post next to the *Gouverneur*), which I took over during the absence of the *Secretair*. . . . My yearly salary is 500 dollars, about 700 Prussian talers. I have had good luck and bad luck, my dear mother, as is usually the case, especially as a merchant.

ing that when three Germans meet they start a Society," [72] and in every large German community there were a wide variety that newcomers could join. Known as *Vereine* (the singular is *Verein*), they ranged from horticulture clubs to political associations. There was the Hamburger Verein, an association of people who came from the town of Hamburg, Germany. There was the Schwaben Verein, a charitable and social club founded by people from Württemberg, Germany. There were many mutual aid societies that provided life insurance, jobless benefits, and medical care. The most well known of these was the Order of the Sons of Hermann. Hermann, the organization's namesake, was a Germanic folk hero whose men defeated three Roman legions at the Battle of Teutoburg Forest in the year A.D. 9.

The Bright Side

With the support of others who had come before or who had arrived at the same time, most immigrants were able to look at the future with optimism. They had to work hard, but not as hard as they would have had to in Germany. Immigrant Johann Pritzlaff wrote home, "You can earn your daily bread better [here] than in Germany; one doesn't live so restrictedly and in such servitude as you do under the great estate-owners." [73]

They liked the fact that they could make progress and leave poverty behind. Christian Kirst wrote during his second year in America:

I've already saved more here and lead a better life with my family than

even the best is able to over there, here you make more in the clear in one year than you can make in debts over there in five years. Here you work hard..., but when it's payday and you get those lovely dollars counted out in your hands, the hardship is forgotten. [74]

Everyone enjoyed America's freedoms. People could go state to state, or across the entire United States, without having to worry about government permits or other paperwork. A family could pack up and move as many times as they wanted and no one cared.

More priceless than the freedom to travel was the freedom to speak out and criticize the government—even the president of the United States—without fear of reprisal. August Blumner wrote to his friends, "I invite you to come over here, should you want to obtain a clear notion of genuine public life, freedom of the people and sense of being a nation. . . . I have never regretted that I came here, and never! never! again shall I bow my head under the yoke of despotism and folly." [75]

In fact, the majority of German immigrants eventually decided that their new country was indeed a land of opportunity, one in which they could fit in without much difficulty. Richard O'Connor writes, "They . . . had a certain steadiness of temperament, a dogged persistence and stolid durability that stood them well in the chanciness of a pioneer's life." [76] Those qualities not only took them far, it helped them make valuable contributions to American society in the years ahead.

CHAPTER FIVE

Real Americans

As the immigrants became more familiar with their new world, they gained confidence, adjusted their goals, and industriously set about earning a living, educating their children, gaining citizenship, and serving their country. Peter Klein wrote of their participation in the Civil War, "Germans have shown themselves to be the keenest defenders of the constitution, and provide entire regiments of the best and bravest of soldiers. . . . They're starting to fill the native Americans with respect." [77]

Becoming a part of American society, coupled with economic changes for the better, made immigrants proud of the communities and the land in which they were achieving so much. As a result, their ties to the Old World weakened. Most remained true to their cultural past—continuing to speak German at home and attending German churches—but in fact they were becoming Americanized in a very real way. As immigrant Carl Schurz expressed it, "I love Germany like my mother and America like my wife. If one must choose, one stays with one's wife, but the love for one's mother lasts a lifetime." [78]

Commitment to Education

The desire to get ahead translated into a desire for education for many immigrants. German culture had a strong commitment to education, and even those immigrants who were uneducated made an effort to improve themselves. They read German-

In one-room schoolhouses they built themselves, German Americans of all ages studied such subjects as English, history, and government.

language newspapers to keep abreast of current events both in Germany and in the United States. Some took classes in American history and government. Many took lessons in the English language.

For some, furthering their education meant a sacrifice of time. For instance, Mathias Dorgathen, a miner who lived in Ohio, took English language classes at night, even after working hard all day. He wrote in 1883, "I'm going to school every evening, with the last teacher I only went to school two evenings a week, but he left, now we've got another teacher, last week he started up evening school again in English, speaking, reading and writing." [79]

For others, it meant using what little money they had for their children's education. If school did not exist in a small German community, the entire population got together, erected a schoolhouse, and hired a teacher. Most took pride in making the building as large and attractive as possible since, in their eyes, it was a reflection of the progressiveness and prosperity of the community.

In larger communities, parents had the option of sending their children to schools established by German Catholic, Lutheran, and Evangelical churches. In these halls of learning, classes were taught in German so that non-English-speaking students would not fall behind in their studies.

Immigrant children in cities could attend public schools, too. Because Germans were so numerous, many public schools included German classes in their curriculum, even teaching it as a part of the foreign-language program to non-Germans. In Chicago in 1900, for instance, authorities estimated that forty thousand pupils, the majority of them non-German, were taking a German class. After a time, however, some Americans opposed such an emphasis on German in the classroom, insisting that learning English was essential to the success of immigrants. Many Germans themselves recognized the wisdom of that argument, and soon schools that had once conducted classes in German switched to English.

The Disadvantages of Learning

As young German Americans learned English, they were able to assimilate more fully into American society. They identified themselves as Americans. They made American friends, played American sports, and went on to American colleges and universities. English became their first language, and their German skills faded. Wilhelm Krumme wrote of his eleven-

Immigrant children in cities became Americanized by attending public schools like this one in New York.

year-old son, "He's a good pupil, that is in the English language since he can handle books fairly well but he doesn't know much German." [80]

Parents were proud of their Americanized offspring, but education and assimilation sometimes had a down side. Children who were Americanized and had a better education were often likely to think that their parents were stupid and out of touch with American ways. Eager to get on with their lives and be as modern as possible, they were often impatient with the older generation's desire to retain ties to the old land, too.

The older generation tried to combat these attitudes, but with little success. One father, Johann Witten, wrote, "Again the German youth suffers temptation from the English [Americans]. Many are nothing but heathens. . . . Anyone who wants to keep his children under control, like I try to, has to watch out very carefully." [81]

Becoming Citizens

Immigrants' children who were born in the United States were proud of the fact that they were American citizens. Many German immigrants were interested in citizenship, too, however. Not only did they feel a great deal of gratitude and loyalty to their new country, but they realized that citizenship officially gave them all the rights and privileges that native Americans enjoyed. For instance, citizens could claim free land under the Homestead Act, but foreigners could not.

Becoming a citizen was relatively easy throughout the 1800s. To qualify, one needed to be white, male, at least twenty-one years of age, and a resident of the United States for five years. For a time, Wisconsin was the exception to the rule; it had a residency requirement of only six months. State leaders argued that the effort an immigrant took when he traveled thousands of miles to start a new life in a new land automatically demonstrated his loyalty and commitment to that land.

Once a man qualified, he could become naturalized. This was a function of state governments until 1906, when the federal government assumed responsibility. Thus, an immigrant usually went to a state court and filled out a declaration of intent to become a citizen. He also provided a witness—usually a close friend—who was willing to swear that the applicant had lived in the United States for five years and that as one 1899 application in New York County, New York, stated, "he has behaved as a man of good moral character, attached to the principles of the Constitution of the United States and well disposed to the good order and happiness of the same." [82]

Often a judge asked the applicant a few simple questions about the government and leaders of the United States. For instance, he could ask the name of the current president or the name of the state's governor. Even if the applicant's answers were wrong, however, a lenient judge often overlooked them and approved the application. The applicant then took an oath renouncing allegiance to Germany and swearing to support the U.S. Constitution; he then became a full-fledged citizen. Records were usually kept of the proceedings, but these could be incomplete or

The children of German immigrants were considered American citizens at birth. They grew up to enjoy all of the privileges that other Americans enjoyed.

full of errors. Thus, no accurate record exists of how many German immigrants became citizens.

Knowledgeable About the Issues

Many of those immigrants who became citizens had no illusions that America's political institutions were perfect. But after having had no say in shaping the government in Germany, many were eager to exercise the privilege of voting in America. And even those who lived through turbulent times, such as the Civil War,

Abraham Lincoln's assassination, and the impeachment of President Andrew Johnson, were pleased to note that the democratic system worked. Johann Bauer wrote home in 1868, "I can't help saying that I feel proud at the thought of being an American citizen. . . . It is a wonderful feeling to realize that you can replace a hateful government with another one." [83]

Once they became citizens, German Americans usually paid careful attention to the issues of the day. Their letters often demonstrated the depth of their understanding and involvement. Bauer wrote home just prior to the Civil War:

There will probably be 4 candidates for *President* in the running. One Republican, one Democrat from the northern states, one Democrat from the southern states, and the 4th will be from the . . . *Knownothings.* . . . The latter party has the principle that foreigners should hold no offices and have to be in the country for 21 years before they are allowed to vote; they won't elect a President all that quickly since the true American believes in the idea that all men are created equal before God, with the same rights. [84]

Although they took an interest in politics and the democratic process, few ordinary German Americans wanted to create a German American party or promote German American special-interest groups. This was because everyone was so varied in background and interest. Agreeing on a unified platform would have been virtually impossible. Instead, most men voted for those candidates who best supported their personal interests. Farmers supported pro-farming candidates. Intellectuals and liberals often supported socialists. Urban residents supported reformers in order to rid themselves of corrupt "city bosses" who controlled some cities in the 1800s.

Unified over Beer

With their varied backgrounds and points of view, there was one element that united Germans when it came to entertainment, home life, politics, and everything else. That was a love of beer. Any political candidate who supported the prohibition of beer or the closure of taverns and beer gardens on Sunday was an enemy of the German community young and old.

Many Americans—particularly churchgoers—viewed beer drinking as wrong, especially on Sunday. German Americans, however, saw beer as one of the undeniable pleasures of life. They also believed that Sunday should be a day of relaxation, when a person could enjoy his family, his music, his food and drink, and his God at the same time. Thus, after German families attended church on a Sunday morning, they went to a neighborhood beer garden or beer hall where they escaped their tiny homes, socialized with their neighbors, and enjoyed the outdoors for a few hours. Beer gardens were more like parks

Although modern beer gardens are tourist attractions, they were once places where German American families relaxed after a long workweek.

than gardens. Author Carl H. Miller describes them:

> Laid out amidst shady trees and sprawling lawns, the typical beer garden was manicured to be the perfect setting for that most important of 19th century pastimes: quaffing [drinking] the amber fluid. . . . There was music, dancing, sport and leisure. It was an occasion for the whole family, and one which usually lasted the entire day, from sunup to sundown. Indeed, for the mostly working class throngs who came, the beer garden was an oasis in an otherwise workaday life. As such, it played an important role in the lives of countless immigrants. [85]

There were some beer gardens that were more elaborate than others. One in Austin, Texas, featured a bubbling spring, fountains, a bowling alley, and a small zoo complete with bears, deer, alligators, and parrots. It also had two outdoor stages for concerts and plays. Pabst Park, sponsored by the Pabst Brewing Company in Milwaukee, was an eight-acre garden complete with a roller coaster and a fun house, and it regularly held Wild West shows. Schlitz Park, also in Milwaukee, had a three-story pagoda-like structure that offered a panoramic view of the city and a garden that was illuminated at night by more than two hundred gaslights.

In every beer garden, tables were set in the shade and a wide variety of food was served, including ham, roast beef, jellied fish, herring salad, potato salad, bean salad, and, in Texas, chili. Usually there was a local German band playing in the background. Sometimes businessmen and social organizations such as singing societies met there. Of course, there was always plenty of beer. "They were mighty fine places," remembered one patron in 1937. "The beer gardens of the old days were places where you went to drink pleasantly, not to get drunk. You took the family along. And the food they had! You don't know what good food is these days!" [86]

Desperate Measures

With beer such an important part of everyone's life, German Americans saw any threat of banning or restricting alcohol as an attack on their civil rights, their cultural freedom, and their leisure time. Occasionally such threats pushed them to take desperate measures. In 1855, when city authorities in Davenport, Iowa, confiscated several barrels of beer, immigrants rioted and reclaimed the brew. In Chicago that same year, the so-called Lager Beer Riots erupted after Mayor Levi D. Boone raised fees for liquor licenses by 600 percent and decreed that beer could not be sold or drunk on Sunday. Thousands of immigrants turned out to demonstrate. They stormed the city hall, attacked police officers, and dispersed only after one of their number was killed. In 1867 New York Germans cooperated with Irish immigrants—traditionally their enemies—to vote down a law that would have closed bars on Sunday.

The passing of the Eighteenth Amendment, known as Prohibition, in 1919 was a severe blow to the German American community, but it did not stop the beer from flowing. When it became illegal to manufacture or sell any alcoholic beverage anywhere in the nation, breweries, beer gardens, and beer halls were forced to close. Like millions of other Americans, however, German Americans continued to drink, buying their beer at the corner speakeasy (illegal bar) or brewing it in their cellars. Miller writes:

> Homebrew, or *heimgemacht* as the Germans called it, became all the rage during Prohibition. Manufacturers of malt syrup (an essential ingredient for homebrewers) reported torrential sale. . . . In some cities, so much homebrew was being made that sewer systems were choked beyond function by the onslaught of spent hops [the plant that gives a characteristic taste to beer]. [87]

When the Nineteenth Amendment repealed Prohibition in 1933, brewing and drinking returned full force in German communities throughout the country. Ludwig Dilger wrote, "Since the 7th of this month [April 1933] our breweries have been going full steam again. They are working 24 hours a day and still can't brew enough beer." [88]

German American Statesmen
German immigrants were united when it came to beer legislation, but as a group, most were not politically active. Nevertheless some immigrants became politicians, serving at all levels, from local school boards to state legislatures to the national cabinet. One of the most noteworthy statesmen was Gustav Koerner, who was born in Frankfurt am Main in Germany and became a member of the Illinois legislature in 1842. He went on to serve as a judge on the Illinois Supreme Court from 1845 until 1851. From 1853 until 1857 he served as lieutenant governor of the state. Another notable was Philip Becker of Oberotterbach, Germany, who became the first foreign-born mayor and the first of eight German American mayors to serve in Buffalo, New York.

Carl Schurz of Missouri served in the Civil War and was the first German American elected to the U.S. Senate.

True Americanism

Carl Schurz first gained national renown for his speech "True Americanism," which was delivered in Boston on April 18, 1859. His theme—America's role in preserving world peace—remains relevant even today. It is excerpted from Charles Rounds's "Carl Schurz," Wisconsin Authors and Their Works.

What is the rule of honor to be observed by a power so strongly and so advantageously situated as this Republic [the United States] is? Of course I do not expect it meekly to pocket real insults if they should be offered to it. But, surely, it should not . . . swagger about among the nations of the world, with a chip on its shoulder, shaking its fist in everybody's face. Of course, it should not tamely submit to real encroachments upon its rights. But, surely, it should not, whenever its own notions of right or interest collide with the notions of others, fall into hysterics and act as if it really feared for its own security and its very independence. As a true gentleman, conscious of his strength and his dignity, it should be slow to take offense. In its dealings with other nations it should have scrupulous regard, not only for their rights, but also for their self-respect. With all its latent resources for war, it should be the great peace power of the world. . . . It should seek to influence mankind, not by heavy artillery, but by good example and wise counsel. It should see its highest glory, not in battles won, but in wars prevented. It should be so invariably just and fair, so trustworthy, so good tempered, so conciliatory, that other nations would instinctively turn to it as their mutual friend and the natural adjuster of their differences, thus making it the greatest preserver of the world's peace. . . .

Is not this good Americanism? It is surely today the Americanism of those who love their country most. And I fervently hope that it will be and ever remain the Americanism of our children and our children's children.

The best-known German immigrant to serve in office in the United States was Carl Schurz, born in Cologne, Germany, in 1829. A Forty-Eighter who became a staunch Republican, he was credited with convincing thousands of German Americans to join the Republican Party prior to the 1860 election. Wisconsin political historian Alexander M. Thompson writes, "He made converts wherever he spoke, and thousands of his nativity [Germans] were won to the true political faith by his eloquent speeches." [89]

To German Americans, Schurz was a symbol of moral leadership and intellectual achievement. His continuing high expectations for himself and all Americans were expressed in the following words: "Ideals are like stars; you will not succeed in touching them with your hands. But like the seafaring man on the desert of waters, you choose them as your guides, and following them you will reach your destiny." [90]

In 1869 Schurz became the first German-born citizen to be elected to the U.S. Senate. He served as a senator from the state of Missouri. In 1877 he was appointed secretary of the interior under President Rutherford B. Hayes. Over the next four years he made significant advances in his department, including formulating a conservation policy, introducing civil service reforms, and making improvements to the Bureau of Indian Affairs.

Serving Their Country

Schurz was still a young man in the 1860s, and along with thousands of young German Americans, he risked his life fighting in the Union army during the Civil War (1861–1864). Like Schurz, most immigrants who enlisted felt gratitude or wanted to prove their loyalty to their new country, and many opposed slavery. Many also remembered the discord that had existed among autonomous German states and were determined to preserve the Union. One soldier remembered, "In this great moment in the history of the United States there were no Irish, no Germans, no Scandinavians, no aliens, but only Americans. . . . All fought like brothers, shoulder to shoulder, for one holy purpose—the preservation of the union." [91]

Germans made up a large proportion of soldiers in the Union army. Out of approximately 2.5 million troops, 750,000 were German American and 216,000 were German born. Thus, they were often allowed to form their own units, elect their own officers, and even speak German among themselves. They were not always the showiest in battle, but they were noted for their neatness, precision, and respect for authority. They fought hard, too, causing even Confederate general Robert E. Lee to note their presence. "Take the Dutch (Deutsche or German) out of the Union Army and we'll whip the Yankees easily," [92] he stated.

Pictured with his wife Mamie, Dwight D. Eisenhower, of Pennsylvania Dutch (German) descent, was elected the thirty-fourth president of the United States.

German immigrants proved their loyalty to America by serving in other wars as well. Although many opposed America's involvement prior to World War I, thousands rushed to serve when war was declared. Their greatest fear was not death, however; rather, it was the fact that they might meet their own families as enemies on the battlefield in France and Germany. "We had cousins and uncles over there (in the American army)," remarked Helen Wagner, who lived in Yorkville, a German neighborhood in New York City. "Lord knows how many of them were nearly killed by my brothers (who had remained in Germany and served in the German army)." [93]

Going to war against Germany in World War II was easier because many young German Americans felt fewer ties to their homeland by then. They also recognized the danger the Nazi regime posed to the world and believed that Adolf Hitler's treatment of German Jews and other minorities was unspeakably inhumane. Of the 11 million soldiers who served in the U.S. armed forces during World War II, one-third were of German ancestry. Even relatively new arrivals, such as Ludwig Hofmeister, who came to the United States in 1925, did their part to defeat the enemy. Hofmeister remembered one man he captured: "There was one big Nazi, and it was a pleasure for me to arrest him. He must have been one of them guys who made himself rich, because he was living very, very, very luxurious. I had no pity on him, because he was a big fat guy, and I didn't like him." [94]

While thousands of Americans of German descent served in the ranks of the U.S. military during World War I and II, there were also hundreds who achieved the prestigious rank of admiral or general. For instance, General Carl Spaatz, a German American who flew combat planes during World War I, was made commander of the U.S. Air Force in Europe in 1943. In 1945 he was put in charge of the final air assault on Japan, a move that helped lead to the end of the war. Admiral Chester Nimitz, whose grandfather immigrated to America in 1844, was commander in chief of the U.S. Pacific Fleet during World War II and was largely responsible for the successes of the U.S. Navy in the Pacific theater during that war. General Dwight D. Eisenhower, of Pennsylvania Dutch (German) descent, served as commander of U.S. Allied forces during World War II, and he devised and carried out the plan for the invasion of Nazi-held Europe. He was later elected the thirty-fourth president of the United States.

Service in the military was only one of the many areas in which German immigrants and their descendants participated in American affairs over the years. From agriculture to the arts, they made their mark, shaping and coloring American culture. As President Bill Clinton stated in 1995, "In the course of 300 years of German [immigration] to this great land, German Americans have attained prominence in all areas of our national life. . . . Many distinguished names cannot begin to summarize all the gifts that [they] have brought to our Nation's history." [95]

CHAPTER SIX

A Powerful Force

As millions of ordinary German Americans became a part of the U.S. population and embraced and embodied American ideals, they became a powerful, constructive force in American society. Their energy and creativity refreshed the economy. Their intelligence and determination helped the United States rise to the top in agriculture and industry throughout the world. Richard O'Connor observes, "German brains, with their obvious aptitude for science, education, and technology, have contributed more than their share to America's unchallenged industrial establishment." [96] Their ambition and perseverance reinforced the American work ethic. Qualities that they believed were important—frugality, respect for authority, patriotism, and love of family—became values that are recognized as quintessentially American.

Other aspects of their culture were assimilated into American society, too. German foods such as hamburgers and hot dogs became American favorites. German innovations such as blue jeans, designed by immigrant Levi Strauss, and ketchup, created and mass produced by German American Henry J. Heinz, are viewed around the world as definitive American products.

Contributions to the Arts

In addition to contributors like Strauss and Heinz, the list of German Americans who have enriched American society is long and impressive. It ranges from business mogul John Jacob Astor to baseball hero Babe Ruth to renowned physicist Albert Einstein. It includes the achievements of families such as the Boeings, the Chryslers, the Firestones, the Fleischmanns, the Guggenheims, and the Weyerhaeusers.

In politics, Secretary of State Henry Kissinger, who was born in Fuerth, Germany, and came to the United States in 1938, is as esteemed as Carl Schurz. Among other accomplishments, Kissinger was awarded the Nobel Peace Prize in 1973 for bringing an end to the Vietnam War. He was also instrumental in brokering an end to the 1973 Yom Kippur War between Israel, Syria, and Egypt. Thomas Nast, who mixed his politics with art, used his editorial cartoons to educate barely literate immigrants about municipal corruption that was all around them. "Nast was one of the greatest statesmen of his time," said publisher J. Henry Harper. "I have never known a man with surer political insight." [97] Two of Nast's most lasting political contributions were the elephant and the donkey that have been used as symbols of the Republican and Democratic Parties over time.

Renowned physicist Albert Einstein, a German Jewish refugee, takes the oath of allegiance to the United States as he is sworn in as an American citizen in 1940.

Nast was not the only German American artist to make a name for himself in America. Dankmar Adler in Chicago and Alexander C. Eschweiler in Milwaukee had an enormous impact on the local architecture of their cities. In Washington, D.C., the Healy Building—the original building of Georgetown University—was designed by German American architects John L. Smithmeyer and Paul J. Pelz. German designer August Gottlieb Schönborn was instrumental in designing the dome of the U.S. Capitol during the 1860s.

Two giants of the field of photography —Alfred Stieglitz and Alfred Eisenstaedt —were German Americans. Herman Herzog and Albert Bierstadt created landscape paintings that hung in museums and galleries from San Francisco to New York City.

In the field of music, impresario Oscar Hammerstein enlivened and modernized American opera. German-born Theodore Thomas, conductor of the New York Philharmonic, gained renown as the first great orchestra conductor in the United States. Due to Thomas's influence, orchestras were established in cities like Philadelphia, Baltimore, Pittsburgh, Cincinnati, and San Francisco, most of them conducted by German Americans.

In the movie industry, Carl Laemmle founded Universal Studios, and actress Marlene Dietrich took Hollywood by storm. Under Laemmle in the late 1910s, Universal became America's leading film producer. Dietrich gained legendary status for her glamour and her roles in movies such as *The Flame of New Orleans* and *Judgment at Nuremberg*.

German actress Marlene Dietrich was a legend in Hollywood for her glamour and talent.

Industry and Technology

With their dedication to success in any field that they tackled, German Americans played a significant role not only in the arts but also in a variety of technological, industrial, and commercial advances and enterprises. Charles Steinmetz, known as "the Wizard of Schenectady," revolutionized the science of electrical engineering. In 1901 Harvard University awarded him an honorary degree as "the foremost electrical engineer in the world," [98] and his work at the General Electric Company in

Rocket Scientist

Wernher von Braun, one of the world's foremost rocket engineers and a leading authority on space travel, came to the United States much later than most German immigrants. Nevertheless his contributions were invaluable. Details of von Braun's life and accomplishments are presented by historian Roger D. Launius on the NASA headquarters Web site.

Wernher von Braun . . . was one of the most important rocket developers and champions of space exploration during the period between the 1930s and the 1970s. As a youth he became enamored [fascinated] with the possibilities of space exploration by reading the science fiction of Jules Verne and H.G. Wells, and from the science fact writings of Hermann Oberth, whose 1923 classic study, *Die Rakete zu den Planetenräumen (By Rocket to Space)*, prompted young von Braun to master calculus and trigonometry so he could understand the physics of rocketry. . . .

[Living in Germany] von Braun [became] well known as the leader of what has been called the "rocket team," which developed the V-2 ballistic missile for the Nazis during World War II. The V-2s were manufactured at a forced labor factory called Mittelwerk. . . . Before the Allied capture of the V-2 rocket complex, von Braun engineered the surrender of 500 of his top rocket scientists, along with plans and test vehicles, to the Americans. For fifteen years after World War II, von Braun [worked] with the United States army in the development of ballistic missiles. . . .

In 1960, his rocket development center transferred from the army to the newly established NASA and received a mandate to build the giant Saturn rockets. Accordingly, von Braun became director of NASA's Marshall Space Flight Center and the chief architect of the Saturn V launch vehicle, the superbooster that would propel Americans to the Moon.

Schenectady, New York, made possible the huge electric generators that today supply power to American homes.

George Westinghouse, born to immigrant parents in 1846, invented railroad devices such as an air brake that prevented collisions and saved thousands of lives. He went on to found the giant Westinghouse Company that still flourishes and has been involved in everything from broadcasting to manufacturing electrical appliances.

Rudolph Wurlitzer and Henry Steinway were notable musical-instrument makers even before making their way to America.

Whereas the former gained fame for his organs and band instruments, the latter focused on pianos. Immigrating to America in 1850, Steinway launched Steinway and Sons piano company and earned the reputation of making some of the finest musical instruments in the world.

"It's a Doozy!"

German Americans became legendary for their contributions in the automobile industry as well. One of the most renowned families, the Studebakers, arrived from Germany during the eighteenth century and became makers of Conestoga-style wagons during the 1850s. Studebaker wagons and carriages won many awards for design and craftsmanship, and prior to 1900 the company was the largest manufacturer of horse-drawn vehicles in the world. In 1902 the Studebakers began building automobiles, which they manufactured for over half a century. The company's slogan, "Give More than You Promised," made their products popular with everyone from farmers to presidents. The Studebaker Company was a leader in automobile manufacturing from 1920 until 1966.

The Duesenbergs were a second German American family who contributed to the auto industry. Brothers Frederick and August immigrated from Lippe, Germany, in 1885; due to their design and manufacturing skill, their name became synonymous with luxury, style, elegance, and precision in automobiles during the 1920s and 1930s. Duesenberg cars were such fine machines that they contributed their name to American slang. The phrase "It's a Doozy!" signified something that was unsurpassed in excellence.

Another highly popular American automobile, the Stutz Bearcat, was created by Harry C. Stutz, born to German American parents in 1876. The Bearcat premiered in 1912 and won numerous racing events due to its powerful engine and efficient transmission. In 1915 famed cross-country driver Ernest G. "Cannonball" Baker drove a Bearcat from San Diego to New York in a record-breaking eleven days, seven hours, and fifteen minutes.

In the 1920s, because of its sporty appearance and powerful engine, the Bearcat became a favorite with well-to-do young people who loved drinking, dancing, and fast cars. It was as much a part of the times as flappers, gangsters, and college men in raccoon-skin coats, and it supplied just as much noise and energy. As journalist Richard A. Wright observes, "Stutz cars helped put the roar in the Roaring Twenties." [99]

The Brewmasters

Another industry in which German Americans made notable contributions was that of beer making. Before the 1840s and 1850s, Americans drank mainly English-style beer—ales and stouts—but with the arrival of beer yeast from Germany in midcentury, the popularity of more well-known types of beers—lagers and golden pilsners, for instance—soared.

With German immigrants drinking millions of gallons of beer annually, it was no wonder that enterprising immigrants like Joseph Schlitz, Adolphus Busch, and others realized that they could make their fortunes establishing and operating breweries in their new homeland. Most started out small. Schlitz, for instance, laid the foundation of his fortune by brewing three barrels of beer a day and peddling them in a wheelbarrow. With millions of eager clientele, however, business boomed. Local breweries became the heart of many German American neighborhoods, employing thousands of immigrants. In 1873 more than four thousand breweries operated in the United States, many of them relatively unknown such as the Jackson Brewery, the J.G. Sohn and Sons Brewery, the Christian Moerlein Brewing Company, and the John Kauffman Brewing Company.

In large breweries, brewmasters—those responsible for the fermentation, storage, and filtration of beer—commanded unmatched respect and enjoyed the status of virtual nobility both inside and outside the workplace. With their wealth and position in the community, they were the embodiment of success in the eyes of ordinary German Americans. And for the ordinary German American, working in a brewery

Horse-drawn delivery trucks carrying barrels of beer leave the Schlitz brewery in Milwaukee. To this day, Schlitz remains one of the best-known names in American beer.

was a valued privilege. Facilities were usually clean and up to date, pay was good, and employment was guaranteed. There could be extra benefits, too. In Milwaukee, beer deliverymen were given an allowance of three dollars a day to spend on beer. Most spent it along their route, where they paid a mere five cents for a glass of brew.

Among so many competitors, the beer barons—as famous brewers such as Schlitz, Busch, and Frederick Pabst were called—owed their success to the fact that they worked tirelessly to create a good product and then marketed it creatively. For instance, Busch, who was headquartered in St. Louis, Missouri, promoted his Budweiser Beer by touring around the country in a luxurious railroad car and handing out distinctive calling cards—gold-plated pocket knives with his face on them.

Pabst and Schlitz, who battled each other for top position in sales all their lives, worked out of their separate headquarters in Milwaukee. One of Pabst's most legendary promotions involved tying blue ribbons around the necks of his Pabst Select Brand beer, which he was selling in virtually every major city in the country. The tactic was so successful that the beer was later renamed Pabst Blue Ribbon Beer. In 1893 Pabst became the first brewer in America to sell more than 1 million barrels of beer in a single year.

Schlitz's slogan, "The Beer That Made Milwaukee Famous," kept his products in top markets for decades as well. The phrase originated after the Great Chicago Fire of 1871 destroyed much of that city, including its breweries and waterworks. Schlitz sent huge shipments of his beer to the desperate (and thirsty) Chicagoans, floating it by shiploads down Lake Michigan. As word of the deed spread, the name Schlitz became famous throughout the country and the world. Schlitz's reputation—and that of other brewmasters—has endured throughout the decades, and due to their influence, lager beer is as American as apple pie and the Fourth of July.

Family Traditions

Although famous individuals and families made significant contributions to America, ordinary German immigrants influenced the country in memorable ways as well. As one writer notes, "The relative handful of famous German-Americans has been far less consequential in the shaping of America than have the anonymous common folk." [100]

One example of this is the all-American practice of relaxing and having fun on Sunday. The German habit of enjoying music, conversation, and good food on sunny Sunday afternoons slowly but surely captured the imagination of American families, who modified their habits to match those of their immigrant neighbors. Former president John F. Kennedy once wrote, "To the influence of the German immigrants in particular we owe the mellowing of the austere Puritan imprint on our daily lives. The Germans clung to their concept of the 'Continental Sunday' as a day . . . of relaxation, of picnics, of visiting, of quiet drinking . . . while listening to the music of a band." [101]

German American holiday traditions were also so colorful and enjoyable that Americans could not resist adopting them. Christmas, as it is observed today, has its

Jolly Old St. Nick

Along with his political and artistic contributions, German American cartoonist Thomas Nast gave America its jolly, red-suited image of Santa Claus. The following excerpt from the "Thomas Nast Portfolio," found on the Web site of the Ohio State University Libraries, explains.

Thomas Nast "invented" the image popularly recognized as Santa Claus. Nast first drew Santa Claus for the 1862 Christmas season *Harper's Weekly* cover . . . to memorialize the family sacrifices of the Union during the early and, for the north, darkest days of the Civil War. Nast's Santa appeared as a kindly figure representing Christmas, the holiday celebrating the birth of Christ. . . . When Nast created his image of Santa Claus he was drawing on his native German tradition of Saint Nicholas, a fourth-century bishop known for his kindness and generosity. In the German Christian tradition December 6 was (and is) Saint Nicholas day, a festival day honoring Saint Nicholas and a day of gift giving. Nast combined this tradition of Saint Nicholas with other German folk traditions of elves to draw his Santa in 1862.

Thomas Nast's depiction of Santa Claus helped popularize the figure in American culture.

roots in the Pennsylvania Dutch celebration of the feast of St. Nicholas, also known as St. Nick. A Christian bishop who lived during the fourth century, St. Nicholas was famous for his generosity, especially to children, and the German custom of giving gifts to children on this saint's day spread throughout America as a result of immigrant observances. Gift givers sometimes put on false beards and tall hats when they distributed presents, becoming forerunners of America's traditional Santa Claus. German families also decorated evergreen trees with candy, fruit, and gingerbread shapes, creating the forerunners to today's Christmas trees.

Easter bunnies, bonnets, and colored eggs also stem from German traditions. In Germany, children looked forward to the arrival of the *Oschter Haws*, a rabbit who laid colored eggs in nests. Little boys used their caps and girls their hats to create nests in a secluded place around the home or garden. Edible Easter bunnies, first created out of pastry and sugar in Germany in the early 1800s, were the forerunners of the candy that children enjoy today on Easter.

A less notable American holiday— Groundhog Day—grew out of the German religious observance of Candlemas, a Christian feast day commemorating the presentation of the infant Jesus in the temple in Jerusalem. According to a Pennsylvania Dutch saying, when a bear saw his shadow on Candlemas (February 2), he would crawl back into his hole for another six weeks of winter. In America, the bear changed into a groundhog over the years. Today, Americans wait for groundhog Punxsutawney Phil to give the official forecast for the arrival of spring when he pokes his head out of his heated burrow in Pennsylvania every February 2.

Labor Unions

Just as immigrants influenced lighthearted aspects of American life, they also had an impact on more serious ones, including conditions in the workplace. In the 1800s workers had few rights when it came to their jobs. Employers had ultimate control, hours were long, and wages were low. Workers suffered injury and oppression in large enterprises like foundries, meatpacking companies, and steel mills, yet few dared complain for fear of losing the little they had.

With the coming of the Forty-Eighters, German Americans enthusiastically began playing active roles both in unions and in organizations that agitated for workers' rights. Often these groups were led by German Socialists and Communists, and their demands were considered extremely radical—elimination of the capitalist system, destruction of the government, and the like. However, groups like the Arbeiter Bund ("Workers' Federation") and the Eight Hour League also pushed for more practical changes, such as shorter workdays and care for older workers. Their efforts led to many reforms that were later incorporated into the Social Security system.

Even into the twentieth century, German Americans played a significant role in improving conditions for the working person. For instance, Walter Reuther, the son of a German activist, was president of the United Auto Workers from 1946 until 1970. In that position of leadership, Reuther fought for rights and benefits for his membership that were unheard of during the early years of unions. Besides salary improvements, workers were given enhanced job security, vacations, benefits, pensions, and unemployment benefits. Thanks to Reuther, work in the auto industry was transformed from a low-wage, part-time job to an occupation that gave its workers a living wage and hope for the future.

The Impact on Education

Another aspect of life that benefited from the German presence in America was that of education. Many immigrants—particularly the Forty-Eighters—had attained high levels of education in Germany. They, and other learned German immigrants, enriched American thought and challenged American colleges to put a greater emphasis on exploring new ideas rather than focusing on time-honored university topics—morals, religion, and the classics. Author Ralph Waldo Emerson testified in 1837, "The German brain is prolific. The sight of the semi-annual catalogue of new publications in Germany is enough to unhinge the strongest mind. The professor must keep abreast with the swelling tide." [102]

Immigrants did not leave their mark on higher education alone. Margarethe

Pictured is a kindergarten class in New York in 1902. The concept of kindergarten was introduced into the American education system by Carl Shurz's wife Margarethe.

Schurz, the wife of immigrant Carl Schurz, was one of many German Americans who believed that early education was vital as well. In Germany, Schurz had studied under kindergarten founder Friedrich Froebel, who believed that children needed supervised interaction with other children so they could learn how to discriminate, analyze, share, and solve problems. Schurz's sister had founded several kindergartens, and Schurz had worked in one of them for a time.

After arriving in Watertown, Wisconsin, with her husband in 1856, Schurz began teaching her own daughter and four neighborhood children games, songs, and group activities selected especially to channel their energy and prepare them for school. Other parents were so impressed with her results that they convinced her to teach their children, too. Shortly thereafter, Schurz opened the first formal kindergarten in America.

Other kindergartens followed. In 1872 the institutions gained the support of the National Education Association, which in 1884 established a department of kindergarten instruction. Due to Schurz and the efforts of many other people, kindergarten became a fundamental element of most public and private schools throughout the United States.

Physical Education

German Americans believed that, while the mind was developing, the body should be well cared for, too. In 1826 immigrant Charles Follen, a professor at Harvard University, became the first to teach gymnastics in the United States. Following in Follen's steps, immigrant Francis Lieber, at Harvard in 1827, was another gymnastics enthusiast.

Both men were part of a movement started by Friedrich Ludwig Jahn, who believed that healthy bodies led to healthy, patriotic minds. Jahn had built the first gymnasium in Berlin, Germany, in about 1809. Like Jahn, both Follen and Lieber were daring pioneers at a time when indoor sports were virtually unheard of in America. A spokesperson for the Iowa Health and Physical Readiness Alliance remarks, "Can you imagine the students [at Harvard], directed by Follen, out on a piece of ground called the Delta, putting together some wood and iron to make bars, ladders and horses, and hanging climbing ropes? How new, weird, and exciting it must have seemed to them." [103]

Follen and Lieber's efforts touched few Americans in the early 1800s. The seeds of the modern physical fitness movement took root in the United States, however, with the arrival of the Forty-Eighters and other immigrants. Also supporters of Jahn, they began creating *Turnvereine* ("exercise associations"), also known as Turner societies. (The German verb *turnen* means "to do gymnastic exercises.") The first, the Cincinnati Central Turner Society, was founded in 1848. By 1850 the association had a membership of 380 boys and 90 girls, all of them German immigrants.

The first Turner hall in New York City opened in 1850. In it and others throughout the country, young men practiced gymnastic skills on parallel bars and

As a result of the popularity of Turner societies in the 1890s, American schools, like this one in New York, began to incorporate physical education into the curriculum.

vaulting horses, and young women developed their strength and dexterity using wooden clubs and poles in choreographed displays. At the height of its popularity in the 1890s, the Turner movement included more than three hundred societies with over forty thousand members nationwide.

Due to the Turners, other educators began to see the benefits of physical education and added such programs to grammar and high school curricula around the country. Although these programs were virtually eliminated during World Wars I and II, the importance of physical fitness and the resurgence of physical fitness programs in the 1960s emphasized the

foresightedness of German Americans of earlier decades.

With such a positive influence on American society, German Americans seemed an unlikely group to experience the intolerance and discrimination that many immigrants faced upon coming to America. Such was not the case, however. At various periods, anti-immigrant feelings and wartime jitters created a hatred for Germans that the immigrants themselves unwittingly aggravated. As they quickly learned, America, for all its good points, had a history of xenophobia (fear and contempt of foreigners) that could flare forth with only the slightest provocation.

CHAPTER SEVEN

"Foreign Malcontents and Misfits"

Despite the welcoming words on the Statue of Liberty—"Give me your tired, your poor, your huddled masses yearning to breathe free"—all immigrant groups faced discrimination when they arrived in the United States. Americans were inclined to scorn newcomers because they were poor. They took advantage of immigrants because they appeared ignorant, and they feared them because they competed for jobs.

Germans were viewed with less suspicion than other immigrants since they were Caucasian, hard working, and quick to adapt. Richard O'Connor writes, "Statistics showed that Germans were among the most preferred nationalities—not necessarily because of their aptitude for citizenship but because of their skill and diligence." [104] Nevertheless, they still inspired anti-immigrant feelings, which were expressed individually and through a range of secret societies such as the Order of United Mechanics, the Order of the Sons of America, the United Daughters of America, the Order of United Americans, and the Order of the Star-Spangled Banner. Author Roger O'Conner, contributor to Bowling Green University's American Culture Studies program, writes:

A Know-Nothing campaign ribbon from 1844 illustrates the group's desire to restrict immigrant participation in American affairs.

The nativist [anti-immigrant] sentiment that existed in the 1890's by no means represented the views of the majority of Americans, many of which were new immigrants themselves. Nevertheless, nativism was characteristic of a significant portion of the population and helps to explain some of the obstacles which confronted the immigrant population. [105]

The Know-Nothings

One of the most notorious and outspoken nativist groups in the United States during the 1850s was the American Party—commonly nicknamed the Know-Nothings because, when asked to give details of their activities, its members replied that they "knew nothing." The party grew out of the Order of the Star-Spangled Banner, founded in New York City in about 1849. Its platform called for restrictions on immigration, for the exclusion of the foreign-born from voting or holding public office in the United States, and for a twenty-one-year residency requirement for citizenship. In their declaration of principles adopted at their first convention, party leaders asserted that Europe was sending "the feeble, the imbecile, the idle, and intractable" to the United States, and they stated that people of foreign birth were of "an ignorant and immoral character," [106] not fit to participate in America's democratic process.

The American Party grew in popularity as a result of the dramatic rise in immigration during the 1850s, coupled with dissatisfaction with conventional political parties such as the Democrats and the Whigs (opponents of the Democratic Party who favored high tariffs and a loose interpretation of the Constitution). Anti-Catholic feelings swelled the ranks of the Know-Nothings as well. Most Americans were Protestants, and the Know-Nothings were afraid that Catholic immigrants would be more loyal to the pope than to the United States. The most radical even believed that Catholics intended to take over the United States and place it under the pope's rule.

A third factor—competition in the workplace—increased the American Party's membership, too. Hardworking immigrant merchants and craftsmen took customers from more established businesses. Immigrants were also willing to work for low wages in factories, mills, and shops, taking American jobs and making it harder for American workers to demand higher pay. Thus, the nativists reasoned that the fewer immigrants there were in the United States, the more opportunities there would be for everyone else.

The American Party attracted more than 1 million members during the 1850s. By the end of 1855, it had carried elections in a dozen states. That same year, more than one hundred congressmen were party members. The party lost popularity and influence during the 1860s due to the Civil War, but the nativist point of view remained alive and well in America, and it was reinforced by the inflammatory words and actions of some of the immigrants themselves.

New Germany

German Americans had never hidden the fact that, although they intended to remain in America permanently, they were extremely proud of their heritage. Some small groups, such as the Giessen Society in Missouri in 1835 and the Adelsverein in Texas in 1842, even came to the United States with the purpose of creating independent, pro-German communities in America. German author Franz Loher, who suggested the creation of such a state somewhere between the Missouri River and the Great Lakes, described what he felt would be its perfect composition:

They [the settlers] will become Americans, good republicans and good businessmen. They will mix with the non-Germans and will intermarry and will assume many of their manners. But the general tenor will remain German through and through. Our people will be able to produce wine on the riverbanks and drink it, accompanied by cheerful songs and dances. They will be able to have German schools and universities, German literature and art, German science and philosophy, German regiments, courts and state assemblies, in short, they will be able to build a German state in which their language will be the official language, just as English is now, and in which the German way of life will live, thrive and predominate exactly as the English way does everywhere now. [107]

German at Heart

Articles such as the following one, which was written by a German American and published in the Cincinnati Volksfreund *newspaper in 1848, emphasized that many immigrants remained German at heart despite outward appearances. The excerpt is from Willi Paul Adams's* The German Americans, *found on the Web site of Indiana University–Purdue University at* www-lib.iupui.edu/kade/adams/toc.html.

Being German-American is a very personal thing. We want and we find external independence here, a free middle-class way of life, uninhibited progress in industrial development, in short, political freedom. To this extent we are completely American. We build our houses the way Americans do, but inside there is a German hearth that glows. We wear an American hat, but under its brim German eyes peer forth from a German face. We love our wives with German fidelity. . . . We live according to what is customary in America, but we hold dear our German customs and traditions. We speak English, but we think and feel in German. Our reason speaks with the words of an Anglo-American, but our hearts understand only our mother tongue. While our eyes are fixed on an American horizon, in our souls the dear old German sky arches upward. Our entire emotional lives are, in a word, German, and anything that would satisfy our inner longing must appear in German attire.

Most German immigrants did not support such radical viewpoints. They failed to take into account, however, that they came across as extremely clannish to mainstream Americans. They lived in German communities, spoke German among themselves, and educated their children in German schools. Most cities had several newspapers in the German language, and these kept their millions of subscribers updated on happenings in Germany. In Kleindeutschland in New York City, at least twenty-eight German-language newspapers existed in 1852. One, the *New Yorker Staats-Zeitung*, had the largest circulation of any German-language paper in the world.

German Americans saw all these elements as important to preserving their culture. Other Americans concluded that the immigrants still identified themselves as Germans, however. They feared that such affection for Germany could easily turn into disloyalty to America if conditions were right.

Socialists and Anarchists

In addition to an unconcealed love of Germany, there were other reasons why

Americans saw German immigrants as potential enemies of the United States. The Forty-Eighters, for instance, had been full-fledged revolutionaries in Germany. They were liberal in their politics and atheists when it came to religion. Confident and opinionated, they never hesitated to express themselves, and sometimes their views were shocking. For instance, in 1855 radical immigrant Karl Heinzen wrote and published a newspaper that called for protection of the working classes from capitalists, the exclusion of religious displays from public life, and the demand for the abolition of the U.S. Senate and the presidency.

Even many ordinary working German Americans were radical enough to make Americans nervous. They supported socialism, a philosophy that opposed capitalism and called for the easing of burdensome and unfair conditions under which the working class suffered. Due to strong German American support, the Socialist movement was particularly strong in New York and in midwestern cities during the late nineteenth and early twentieth centuries. In 1916, for instance, the mayor of Milwaukee and twenty-one of the twenty-five members of its city council were Socialists. Many members of the numerous Turner societies throughout the

A group of female Socialists marches through the streets of New York. The Socialist movement in New York attracted many German Americans.

country were Socialists as well, making Americans suspicious that these apparently innocent gymnasiums were the homes of radicals planning treason.

German American radicals were not content to simply write articles and go to meetings, either. Joined by anarchists, who believed that all forms of government were oppressive and undesirable and should be abolished, they sometimes stirred up trouble in the workplace, instigating strikes and demonstrations, and calling for violence. The following paragraph, published in 1885 in *The Alarm*, a Chicago anarchist manifesto, demonstrates their enthusiasm for bloodshed:

> Dynamite! . . . Stuff several pounds of this sublime stuff into an inch pipe . . . plug up both ends, insert a cap with a fuse attached, place this in the vicinity of a lot of rich loafers who live by the sweat of other people's brows, and light the fuse. A most cheerful and gratifying result will follow. A pound of this good stuff beats a bushel of ballots all hollow. [108]

The Haymarket Square riot in Chicago in 1886 was one notorious episode that seemed to illustrate the dangers of German American radicalism. On May 3, during a demonstration of striking workers at the McCormick Reaper Company, police shot several men. A protest was held the next day at nearby Haymarket Square, led by angry German American anarchists. When the police attempted to disperse the crowd, a riot ensued and a bomb was thrown. Seven police officers were killed and sixty were injured.

Although no one could prove who threw the bomb, eight anarchists—six of them German—were arrested and found guilty. Historian Carl Smith summarizes the state's arguments, which also expressed the public's point of view: "These evil and cowardly agitators were part of a large criminal organization of foreign malcontents and misfits who had together carefully planned riot and murder for no motive other than their hatred of honestly earned property." [109]

"Ambivalence Is the Word"

Anti-German feeling ran high at times during the 1800s, but it was nothing compared to the emotions that were expressed by Americans at the beginning of World War I. In the months preceding the war, Germany under Kaiser Wilhelm II and Chancellor Otto von Bismarck carried out a policy of military proliferation that was alarming not only to its neighbors but also to the United States. German Americans, however, saw the buildup as reasonable and insisted that America should remain neutral in any war that might break out. Even those who were not actively pro-German pushed for neutrality because of their reluctance to take a stand against their homeland.

When Germany went to war against France, Britain, Russia, and other European countries in August 1914, some German Americans vocally defended its war policy, convinced that their homeland was simply responding to an attack. This belief stemmed from articles that they had read in German American newspapers and from propaganda spread by pro-German organizations such as the National German-American Alliance. The alliance had been formed in 1901 by German sympathizer Charles J. Hexamer and claimed a membership of 2 million German Americans.

German Americans were also influenced by letters from their families in Germany, who tried to justify the war. For instance, immigrant Hermann Hagedorn's father, a high official in the German government, wrote, "We have been basely betrayed. Long ago everything was prepared by our foes for the assault upon us at this time." [110] Even though Hagedorn knew the facts and was loyal to America, he felt torn between a desire to side with his father and a knowledge that his homeland was in the wrong: "Soberly gratified though I might be at every German setback, every German victory set my Teutonic [German] heart beating a little faster. Ambivalence is the word for it . . . it made for tension and a feeling of guilt." [111]

German American Internment

When America finally joined the war effort in January 1917, Americans were convinced that the majority of German immigrants were spies and saboteurs,

Beware of Spies

At the request of the U.S. Department of Justice, the following notice, entitled "Beware of Spies and Alien Enemies," was posted in the Los Angeles area during World War I. The notice, which ran in the Los Angeles Times *on January 6, 1918, can be accessed on Raymond K. Cunningham's Web site at* http://netfiles.uiuc.edu/rcunning/www/01061801.htm.

*D*on't tell what you know or hear to strangers. Enemy agents are seeking information *everywhere.* They will try to gain your good graces, falsely impress you with their loyalty and entrap you into giving them information.

Don't discuss military affairs, the number, location and movement of troops with strangers or foreigners.

If you have a son, husband, brother or friend in the U.S. Army *don't* make known the content of his letters to these strangers or foreigners.

Whenever any suspicious or disloyal act comes to your notice don't fail to *immediately report* same . . .

Your want of *care* and *promptness* in this direction may aid the enemy and lead to the loss of American lives.

Secrecy and Alertness means Safety

German American women in New York are fingerprinted as part of the government's effort to register all German aliens during World War I.

ready to do the bidding of the German government. As proof, they pointed to many older German Americans who had never become citizens and thus were, in fact, enemy aliens. (Most had simply neglected to go through the formality of naturalization earlier in the century when they had immigrated.) They also noted that some German Americans had been openly critical of the United States, had taken part in antiwar demonstrations, and had even helped raise hundreds of thousands of dollars for German war victims.

The U.S. government did not agree that most German Americans were disloyal, but it quickly responded to head off possible fifth-column activities—acts of espionage or sabotage that would help the enemy. President Woodrow Wilson announced restrictions on all aliens' rights and movements, including exclusions from areas around forts, arsenals, and airports. Aliens were also banned from owning firearms, entering the District of Columbia, and going up in airplanes or observation balloons. Violations could result in arrest and imprisonment.

Efforts had been made to register all German aliens before the war, and those who were considered most dangerous were arrested almost immediately. Grounds for seizure ranged from making pro-German statements to publishing German American newspapers that endorsed the German war effort. Once arrested, the detainees were locked up in special military prisons throughout the country. A journalist from a New York newspaper described security at the largest prison, located at Fort Oglethorpe, Georgia, which could hold as many as three thousand inmates: "The prison contains three rows of barbed wire that enclosed the barracks. Placed at intervals along the barbed wire are twelve elevated sentry boxes with each box armed with a repeating shot gun, a rifle, and a machine gun." [112]

Conditions were stark in these camps, although a Swiss task force, responsible for German interests in the United States, inspected them to ensure they were humane. Prisoners were supplied plenty of army food and were allowed to read, listen to music, play sports, and hold worship services. Nevertheless, their freedom was curtailed, and most felt the imprisonment was unjust.

Anti-German Hysteria

While the government took legal steps against those it considered dangerous, ordinary Americans reacted in more emotional ways. Patrons removed anything related to Germany from library shelves. Public schools canceled German-language classes. Orchestras refused to play German music. Restaurants renamed sauerkraut "liberty cabbage" and frankfurters and wieners became "hot dogs."

At times, public reaction led to violence. German stores were vandalized. Germans with draft deferments were tarred and feathered. German ministers were threatened if they held services in German. Immigrant Helen Wagner remembered, "You couldn't walk the street with a German paper under your arm. You'd be abused from one end of the block to the other. They went so far they abused poor little German dogs [such as dachshunds and schnauzers] that walked the street." [113]

The most dramatic incident took place near East St. Louis, Illinois, when coal miner Robert P. Prager was hung by a mob of five hundred men and boys who believed he was hoarding explosives. The leaders of the lynch mob were tried, but when their defense counsel called their offense "patriotic murder," [114] a jury agreed and returned a not-guilty verdict.

To counteract such hostility, German Americans tried to show their loyalty in any way they could. Many joined the military. Others bought war bonds. Most stopped speaking German in public places. German proprietors closed beer halls and beer gardens. German communities changed names of streets, buildings, and companies. In the Over-the-Rhine neighborhood, Bremen Street became Republic Street, and German Street became English Street. The officers of German Mutual Insurance renamed their company the Hamilton County Mutual Fire Insurance Company and translated its constitution, bylaws, and signs into English.

When the war ended, many German Americans continued to let their ethnic ties remain buried. Some did this because they had become completely Americanized. Others feared further discrimination if they renewed subscriptions to German American newspapers and returned to German-speaking churches. As one historian explains:

World War I . . . virtually banished ethnic consciousness among German Americans so that the postwar generation suffered from a kind of "cultural amnesia": parents who were immigrants or first-generation Americans had—out of fear and humiliation—so denied their roots that their children grew up with no sense of their own German heritage. [115]

The German American Bund

After World War I most German Americans were extremely cautious about expressing themselves on controversial issues. Nevertheless, there were a few who resented the humiliation Germany had undergone during and after World War I and were not afraid to say so. As Adolf Hitler and his National Socialist German Workers Party—otherwise known as the Nazi Party—rose to power during the 1930s, some of these German supporters responded to Hitler's nationalist words and decided that America would be better off if it were run by the Nazis as well.

In March 1936 they took action. A party of Nazi sympathizers met in Buffalo, New York, and organized the Amerikadeutscher Volksbund ("German American Bund"), whose purpose was to bring Nazism to the United States. Fritz Kuhn, a native of Munich, Germany, was chosen as its leader. The organization quickly attracted many German Americans, who preferred to be called "Germans in America." At its peak, the party had an estimated sixty-five hundred active members and another twenty thousand sympathizers.

Bund rallies were notable for their swastikas (emblems of the Nazi Party), brown uniforms, Nazi salutes, and German songs. Members spouted Hitler's anti-Semitic (anti-Jewish) rhetoric, and distributed pro-Aryan pamphlets praising the blond-haired, blue-eyed physical ideal of Nazi Germany. They supported radical radio commentator Father Charles Coughlin, who verbally attacked prominent Jewish figures during his programs. They campaigned against Franklin Delano Roosevelt during the 1936 presidential election, charging him with being part of a Jewish-Communist conspiracy to take over the world. A few members even used violence against Jewish Americans and Jewish-owned businesses.

Reaction to the Bund

The bund received guidance and financial support from the German government for a time, but the party was never well organized or extremely large. Its largest rally occurred in New York's Madison Square Garden in February 1939, when twenty thousand participants chanted "Heil Hitler" and listened to speakers praising Hitler and denouncing Roosevelt and Secretary of the Treasury Henry Morgenthau Jr. (who was Jewish).

The organization attracted attention and raised the fears of ordinary Americans,

German American bund party members salute the swastika during a rally in February 1939 at New York's Madison Square Garden.

however, even those of German descent. Aileen Lampel Novick, a young German Jew who lived in Queens, New York, during the 1930s, later described her feelings regarding the bund's activities in her neighborhood:

I remember the Saturday evenings when soapboxes were set up on Myrtle Avenue, the main thoroughfare, with orators spewing Father Coughlin diatribes [verbal attacks] and other anti-Semitic hatred while I tried to blend into the crowd. I also remember the brownshirts marching through the streets with swastika flags, and the shock when the restaurant owner on our block was incarcerated as a German-American Bund leader after the United States entered World War II. [116]

The bund caught the attention of the U.S. government during the summer of 1937. Rumors had spread that Kuhn had two hundred thousand men ready to take

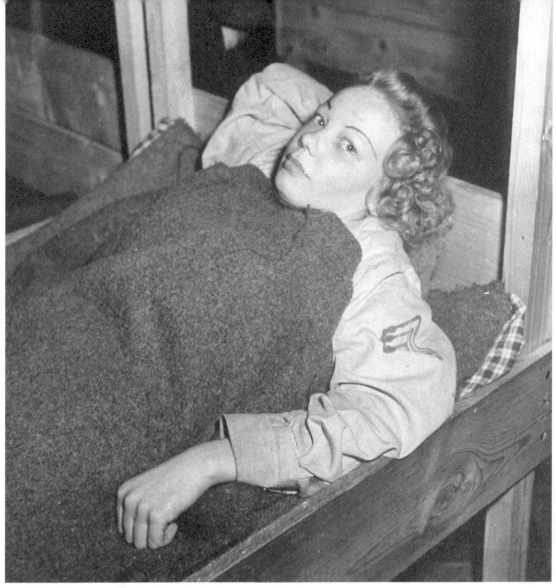

A German American woman suspected of being a Nazi sympathizer lies on her bunk in an American internment camp during World War II.

up arms, so the Federal Bureau of Investigation (FBI) launched an investigation of the organization. In 1939 Kuhn was found to have embezzled bund funds; he was tried, convicted, and sent to a government internment camp in Texas. In 1946 he was deported to Germany.

After the United States declared war on Germany on December 12, 1941, federal officials began to arrest other bund officials as well. Some committed suicide before they could be detained, but twenty-four were caught, tried, convicted of conspiracy, and sentenced to prison. Some bund members had their naturalization revoked, and others spent time in internment camps, but most were left alone after the organization disbanded in 1941.

Internment Again!

In addition to bund arrests, as the United States entered World War II, FBI director J. Edgar Hoover gave the order to arrest all German aliens, American citizens sympathetic to Germany, and persons of German descent whose citizenship was unknown. Almost eleven thousand were placed in internment camps along with other potentially dangerous groups, such as Japanese Americans and Italian Americans. Like the Japanese and Italians, most German American detainees were loyal to the United States. They had simply been engaged in a questionable activity or were in the wrong place at the wrong time. Karl Vogt, who was arrested because he sent money to a relative in Germany, remembered his days in a camp in Oklahoma:

Men were interned for many reasons. Most were German nationals who were in the U.S. for a variety of reasons at the outbreak of the war. Some were visiting professors, some were students, and some were on the crews of ships. Some were there [in camp] because of the ill will of neighbors or business associates. It was easy to accuse someone of being a Nazi! One Lutheran pastor was interned because he had objected to putting the Christian and American flags in the church. . . . He was labeled un-American and reported. [117]

Despite bund activities and government internment camps, public hostility toward German Americans was much reduced during World War II. This was largely because most German immigrants had completely assimilated into American society by this time. Many had moved out of German American communities and worked for mainstream businesses throughout the country. Millions of young German Americans had joined the military in order to fight against Germany. New immigrants who were coming to the United States from Germany about this time were fleeing persecution from the Nazi regime, too. Questioning their loyalty and treating them as enemies would have been both unreasonable and traumatic for them and their families.

Thus, despite wartime hysteria and unfair internment, most German Americans were confident that they were safe and had come to be accepted in their new country. Some had suffered, but the majority was much better off than it had ever been in the Old World. As Ludwig Dilger once observed, "All in all, I've been a citizen of this country [the United States] for 42 years, and this is my home and that of my family. I wish Germany happiness and prosperity, but I never want to live there again." [118]

CHAPTER EIGHT

Remembering a Proud Heritage

By the second half of the twentieth century, the majority of German Americans felt no emotional or spiritual ties to the old country. Germany itself had been divided by the Iron Curtain at the end of World War II, with the Soviet Union shaping the east into a Communist nation. Europe and the United States had rebuilt the rest into a pro-Western democracy. When the two halves had reunited again in 1990, the resulting modern nation bore little resemblance to the country the immigrants had known and loved. Their children and grandchildren—born and raised in the United States—felt only the mildest interest in what went on there.

Then author Alex Haley published his epic novel *Roots* in 1976. In it, he traced his ancestry from Africa through the tribulations and triumphs of seven generations in America. His work, and the television miniseries that followed, drew America's attention to the fact that everyone's ancestry was worthy of note, whether one's family hailed from Africa, England, or Germany.

As a result, many Americans began to try to fill in the blanks on their family trees. They also began to learn about the countries and the cultures from which

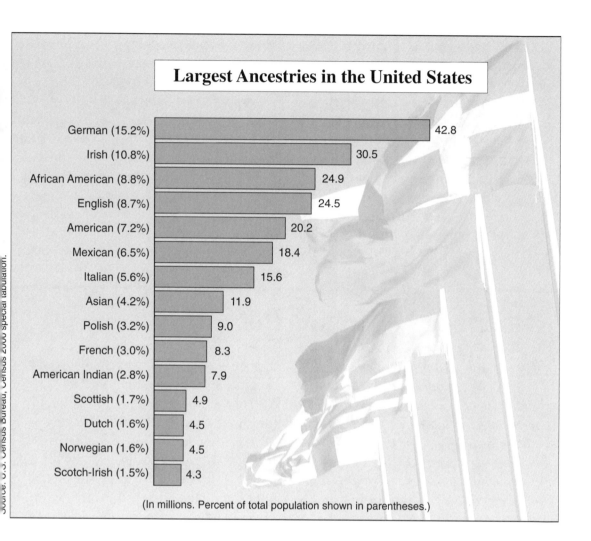

Largest Ancestries in the United States

Ancestry	Millions
German (15.2%)	42.8
Irish (10.8%)	30.5
African American (8.8%)	24.9
English (8.7%)	24.5
American (7.2%)	20.2
Mexican (6.5%)	18.4
Italian (5.6%)	15.6
Asian (4.2%)	11.9
Polish (3.2%)	9.0
French (3.0%)	8.3
American Indian (2.8%)	7.9
Scottish (1.7%)	4.9
Dutch (1.6%)	4.5
Norwegian (1.6%)	4.5
Scotch-Irish (1.5%)	4.3

(In millions. Percent of total population shown in parentheses.)

their ancestors had originated. They traced their forebears' journeys to the New World and found where their families had settled once they arrived. They gained insight into the immigrant way of thinking, and in the process they gained a clearer sense of their own place in the world.

For nearly 43 million Americans of German ancestry, this examination of the past was foreign to their way of thinking. World Wars I and II had taught them that links of any kind to a foreign land could be dangerous. After that devastating time, they had embraced the time-honored notion of America as a melting pot—a vessel in which metals are melted together into a new compound, which has greater strength than its individual elements. They had become Americans. Trying to be anything else seemed wrong. Richard O'Connor observes, "There is nothing more startling to a German-American than a blunt question as to . . . how he might differ from a person of English origin, or an Irishman, or even a Pole or Italian. He feels no difference, and if anything resents the question." [119]

A Tolerance for Differences

Despite this conservative point of view, cultural pluralism—toleration for people of different faiths and ethnicities—became a fact of life in America after 1980. The government commemorated minority leaders like Cesar Chavez and Martin Luther King Jr. with national holidays and postage stamps. Mainstream grocery stores began to carry Korean, Chinese, Mexican, and other ethnic foods. During the holiday season, Jewish Americans celebrated Hanukkah, and African Americans observed Kwanzaa, a holiday that reflected their cultural roots.

Supporters of pluralism believed that American culture was richer because of this way of thinking. Instead of a melting pot, they saw it as a patchwork quilt or a beef stew, where the ingredients retained their identity but were subtly changed by the presence of the different ones. In other words, Americans could retain their cultural, religious, and ethnic roots; be rec-

America, the Melting Pot

The metaphor of America as a melting pot is a traditional one in the United States. As Laura Laubeová points out in an article entitled "Melting Pot vs. Ethnic Stew," found on the Internet at www.tolerance.cz/default.htm, the comparison dates back to J. Hector St. John de Crèvecoeur who immigrated to America from France.

The history of the melting pot theory can be traced back to 1782 when J. Hector [St. John] de Crèvecoeur, a French settler in New York, envisioned the United States not only as a land of opportunity but as a society where individuals of all nations are melted into a new race of men, whose labours and posterity will one day cause changes in the world. The new nation welcomed virtually all immigrants from Europe in the belief that the United States would become, at least for whites, the "melting pot" of the world. . . . A major influx of immigrants occurred mainly after the 1830s, when large numbers of British, Irish, and Germans began entering, to be joined after the Civil War by streams of Scandinavians and then groups from eastern and southern Europe as well as small numbers from the Middle East, China, and Japan. Before the outbreak of World War I in 1914, the American public generally took it for granted that the constant flow of newcomers from abroad, mainly Europe, brought strength and prosperity to the country. The metaphor of the "melting pot" symbolized the mystical potency of the great democracy, whereby people from every corner of the earth were fused into a harmonious and admirable blend.

Dressed in traditional German clothes, this American couple in Sparta, New Jersey, celebrates Octoberfest with a few steins of lager.

ognized and appreciated; and yet remain loyal to America and give it strength at the same time.

Supporting this argument, some German Americans began to examine the heritage that had been put aside by their parents and grandparents. They, too, began studying genealogy, tracing their family tree in libraries, on the Internet, and by talking to members of the older generation. Some traveled to Wisconsin, Pennsylvania, and even Germany and Russia to uncover their roots. Hiller Goehring, who went to his grandfather's village in the Ukraine, unexpectedly met a long-lost second cousin during his travels. "It was such a thrill because when we were growing up, we were told that these people who had stayed behind in Russia were dead, all dead," he recalls. Seeing another country helped Goehring gain a greater appreciation for the United States, too. "When I came home from the trip, I was a better American," he says. [120]

There were other ways that German Americans learned about their roots, too. Some began taking German-language classes. Some attended German cultural clubs and societies that offered activities such as cooking, dancing, and German conversation. These societies also held traditional German festivals—Oktoberfests ("October Festivals"), Sommerfests ("Summer Festivals"), and Volkfests ("Folk Festivals")—complete with German food, beer, and music to attract and educate people of all backgrounds.

Recognizing German Contributions

Genealogy, clubs, and festivals were individual and community recognition of America's German past. The government did its part, too; in 1983 President Ronald Reagan announced that the United States would celebrate the three-hundredth anniversary of German settlement in America. To mark the occasion, the U.S. Postal Service issued a twenty-cent stamp entitled "German Immigration Tricentennial." It bore the image of the sailing ship *Con-*

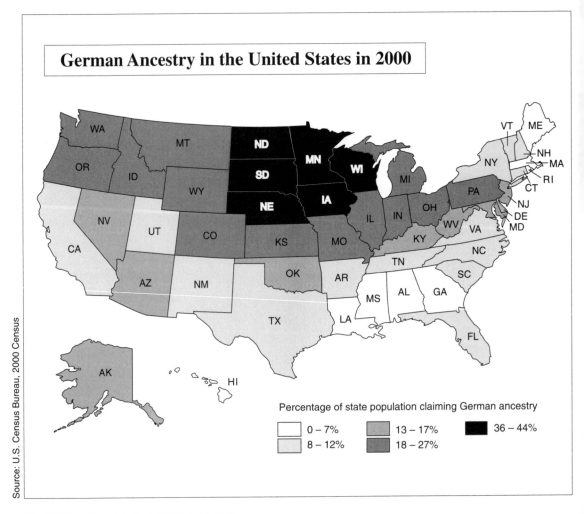

Source: U.S. Census Bureau, 2000 Census

German Ancestry in the United States in 2000

Percentage of state population claiming German ancestry

0 – 7%	13 – 17%
8 – 12%	18 – 27%
	36 – 44%

Two German American women celebrate their heritage during a 1999 parade in New York City honoring a Prussian general who fought in the American Revolution.

cord on which some of the first immigrants traveled to the New World. "[Since 1683], more than seven million German immigrants have entered the United States and made extraordinary human, economic, political, social, and cultural contributions to the growth and success of our great country," [121] Reagan noted on January 20, when he made the announcement.

Five years later Reagan officially proclaimed October 6 German American Day and urged the country to commemorate the event with appropriate ceremonies and activities. Since then, every president has recognized the date. In 1997 President Bill Clinton issued a press statement reiterating Reagan's original words: "All Americans have benefited greatly from the labor, leadership, talents, and vision of Germans and German-Americans, and it is fitting that we set aside this special day to acknowledge their many contributions to our liberty, culture, and democracy." [122]

Ensuring the Vitality of Democracy

Despite their renewed interest in ethnic and cultural roots in America, the children, grandchildren, and great-grandchildren of the German immigrants still see America, and America alone, as their homeland. The majority feels no particular desire to visit a beer hall, listen to a German polka, or own a pair of lederhosen (traditional knee-length pants). Most German Americans do not want to travel to Germany any more than they would like to visit England or Australia. Their heritage as Americans is more important to them than any German roots they may have.

Nevertheless, many retain the basic qualities that were so important to their forebears—a love of family, a dedication to hard work, and a determination to be free. And like their forebears, they steadily and reliably support their communities and their country. As President George H.W. Bush stated on German American Day in 2001, "They will continue their noble role in helping to ensure the vitality of our democracy." [123]

NOTES

Introduction: Three Hundred Years of Immigration

1. Francis Daniel Pastorius, "Pastorius's Description of Pennsylvania, 1700," Early Americas Digital Archive, 2004. www.mith2.umd.edu:8080/eada/html/display.jsp?docs=pastorius_description.xml&action=show.
2. Philip Taylor, *The Distant Magnet: European Emigration to the U.S.A.* New York: Harper and Row, 1971, p. 42.
3. Oscar Handlin, *A Pictorial History of Immigration.* New York: Crown, 1972, p. 327.
4. Quoted in Richard O'Connor, *The German-Americans: An Informal History.* Boston: Little, Brown, 1968, p. 456.
5. Robert E. Ward, "From Germantown to Cleveland in Historical Perspective," Federation of German American Societies of Greater Cleveland, 2004. www.fogas.org/history4.htm.

Chapter One: Life in the Old Country

6. Willi Paul Adams, *The German Americans: An Ethnic Experience*, Indiana University–Purdue University. www-lib.iupui.edu/kade/adams/chap2.html.
7. Gerhard Rempel, "The Thirty-Years War," Western New England College, 2000. http://mars.acnet.wnec.edu/~grempel/courses/wc2/lectures/30yearswar.html.
8. O'Connor, *The German-Americans*, p. 35.
9. Quoted in Howard B. Furer, ed., *The Germans in America: 1607–1970.* Dobbs Ferry, NY: Oceana, 1973, p. 110.
10. Quoted in Gerald Wilk, *Americans from Germany.* New York: German Information Center, 1976, p. 47.
11. Else Conrad, "Else Conrad on the Living Conditions of Workers' Families in Muenchen," 1909, ZUM-Internet. www.zum.de/psm/dormann/dormann46e.php.
12. Quoted in German Americana, "The German 1848 Revolution: A German Perspective," January 2, 1997. www.serve.com/shea/germusa/perspekt.htm.
13. Walter D. Kamphoefner, Wolfgang Helbich, and Ulrike Sommer, eds., *News from the Land of Freedom: German Immigrants Write Home.* Ithaca, NY: Cornell University Press, 1988, p. 573.
14. Quoted in Kamphoefner, Helbich, and Sommer, *News from the Land of Freedom*, p. 465.
15. Moritz Bromme, "The Worker Moritz Bromme Describes His Family's Living Conditions," 1905, ZUM-Internet. www.zum.de/psm/dormann/dormann45e.php.
16. Quoted in Richard H. Zeitlin, "Germans in Wisconsin," State Historical Society of Wisconsin, 1977. http://

home.dwave.net/~dhuehner/germanwis.html.

17. Quoted in Kamphoefner, Helbich, and Sommer, *News from the Land of Freedom*, pp. 164–65.

18. Timothy J. Hatton, "The Age of Mass Migration: What We Can and Can't Explain," Kingston University, 1999. http://ecocomm.anu.edu.au/people/info/hatton/Kingston.pdf.

19. Quoted in Taylor, *The Distant Magnet*, p. 73.

20. Quoted in O'Connor, *The German-Americans*, p. 70.

Chapter Two: The Voyage to America

21. Quoted in Kamphoefner, Helbich, and Sommer, *News from the Land of Freedom*, p. 303.

22. Quoted in Kamphoefner, Helbich, and Sommer, *News from the Land of Freedom*, p. 323.

23. Quoted in Zeitlin, "Germans in Wisconsin."

24. Quoted in Taylor, *The Distant Magnet*, p. 108.

25. Quoted in Kamphoefner, Helbich, and Sommer, *News from the Land of Freedom*, p. 323.

26. Quoted in American Park Network, "Statue of Liberty National Monument History: The Immigrant Journey," 2001. www.americanparknetwork.com/parkinfo/sl/history/journey.html.

27. Quoted in Carol Gohsman Bowen, ed., "Emigration from Hamburg," Mecklenburg WorldGenWeb, 2001. http://blacklake.biz/meck/hambrg.htm.

28. William Bell, "Letters from Perth, Upper Canada: Letter IV," Lanark County Genealogical Society, 2004. http://globalgenealogy.com/LCGS/articles/A-HINT04.HTM.

29. Quoted in Taylor, *The Distant Magnet*, p. 131.

30. Quoted in Spartacus Educational, "Journey to America," 2002. www.spartacus.schoolnet.co.uk/USAEjourney.htm.

31. Quoted in American Park Network, "Statue of Liberty National Monument History."

32. Taylor, *The Distant Magnet*, p. 139.

Chapter Three: All Ashore!

33. Quoted in Kamphoefner, Helbich, and Sommer, *News from the Land of Freedom*, p. 340.

34. Quoted in American Park Network, "Statue of Liberty National Monument History."

35. Quoted in Barbara Krasner-Khait, "If Not Through New York, Then Where?" Family Chronicle, May/June 1999. http://familychronicle.com/NotThroughNY.html.

36. Quoted in University of Waterloo, "1832 Emigrants Handbook for Arrivals at Quebec," 2003. http://ist.uwaterloo.ca/~marj/genealogy/emigrants1832.html.

37. Quoted in Kamphoefner, Helbich, and Sommer, *News from the Land of Freedom*, p. 537.

38. Quoted in Sylvia Payne Higgins Web Site, "Castle Garden," *New York Times*, December 23, 1866. http://

genealogy.about.com/gi/dynamic/
offsite.htm?site=http%3A%2F%
2Fmembers.tripod.com%2F%7E
Silvie%2FCastleGarden.html.

39. Quoted in National Park Service, "The First Gateway—Castle Garden, Ellis Island, and Westward Expansion," January 1992. www.nps.gov/jeff/castle_garden.html.

40. Quoted in Kamphoefner, Helbich, and Sommer, *News from the Land of Freedom*, p. 372.

41. Quoted in Spartacus Educational, "German Immigration," 2002. www.spartacus.schoolnet.co.uk/USAEgermany.htm.

42. Taylor, *The Distant Magnet*, p. 125.

43. Quoted in Furer, *The Germans in America*, p. 118.

44. Quoted in Furer, *The Germans in America*, p. 117.

45. Quoted in Kamphoefner, Helbich, and Sommer, *News from the Land of Freedom*, pp. 356–57.

46. Quoted in Kamphoefner, Helbich, and Sommer, *News from the Land of Freedom*, p. 209.

47. Quoted in Adams, *The Germans in America*.

48. Quoted in iRhine.com, "History of Over-the-Rhine: The Neighborhood," 2004. www.irhine.com/index.jsp?page=history_neighborhood5.

49. Quoted in iRhine.com, "History of Over-the-Rhine."

50. San Antonio Conservation Society, "King William Area," 2004. www.saconservation.org/tours/sitevisits_kingwilliam.htm.

51. Quoted in Kamphoefner, Helbich, and Sommer, *News from the Land of Freedom*, p. 306.

Chapter Four: Newcomers in a New World

52. Quoted in Kamphoefner, Helbich, and Sommer, *News from the Land of Freedom*, p. 323.

53. Quoted in Kamphoefner, Helbich, and Sommer, *News from the Land of Freedom*, p. 493.

54. Quoted in Kamphoefner, Helbich, and Sommer, *News from the Land of Freedom*, pp. 472–73.

55. Quoted in Kamphoefner, Helbich, and Sommer, *News from the Land of Freedom*, p. 484.

56. Quoted in Zeitlin, "Germans in Wisconsin."

57. Quoted in Kamphoefner, Helbich, and Sommer, *News from the Land of Freedom*, p. 596.

58. Quoted in Kamphoefner, Helbich, and Sommer, *News from the Land of Freedom*, p. 76.

59. Quoted in Kamphoefner, Helbich, and Sommer, *News from the Land of Freedom*, p. 342.

60. Quoted in Kamphoefner, Helbich, and Sommer, *News from the Land of Freedom*, p. 154.

61. Quoted in Kamphoefner, Helbich, and Sommer, *News from the Land of Freedom*, pp. 425–26.

62. Quoted in Doris Weatherford, *Foreign and Female: Immigrant Women in America, 1840–1930*. New York: Schocken, 1986, p. 122.

63. Quoted in Weatherford, *Foreign and Female*, p. 150.

64. Quoted in Kamphoefner, Helbich, and Sommer, *News from the Land of Freedom*, p. 132.

65. Quoted in Butler Co. NEGenWeb, "Roots, Branches and Twigs—History of the Family Melvin D. Frahm," 1999. www.rootsweb.com/~nebutler/frahm.html.

66. Quoted in Kamphoefner, Helbich, and Sommer, *News from the Land of Freedom*, p. 60.

67. Quoted in Kamphoefner, Helbich, and Sommer, *News from the Land of Freedom*, p. 161.

68. Quoted in Kamphoefner, Helbich, and Sommer, *News from the Land of Freedom*, p. 582.

69. Quoted in Kamphoefner, Helbich, and Sommer, *News from the Land of Freedom*, p. 177.

70. Quoted in Kamphoefner, Helbich, and Sommer, *News from the Land of Freedom*, p. 483.

71. Quoted in Kamphoefner, Helbich, and Sommer, *News from the Land of Freedom*, p. 87.

72. Quoted in Jeff Hoffman, "Putting Down Roots." www.jeffhoffman.net/roots.htm.

73. Quoted in Kamphoefner, Helbich, and Sommer, *News from the Land of Freedom*, p. 306.

74. Quoted in Kamphoefner, Helbich, and Sommer, *News from the Land of Freedom*, p. 478.

75. Quoted in Kamphoefner, Helbich, and Sommer, *News from the Land of Freedom*, p. 103.

76. O'Connor, *The German-Americans*, p. 183.

Chapter Five: Real Americans

77. Quoted in Kamphoefner, Helbich, and Sommer, *News from the Land of Freedom*, p. 402.

78. Quoted in *Scriptorium*, "Germans Helped Build America—and How Has America Repaid Them?" 2004. www.wintersonnenwende.com/scriptorium/english/archives/germanamerica/ghba03.html.

79. Quoted in Kamphoefner, Helbich, and Sommer, *News from the Land of Freedom*, p. 452.

80. Quoted in Kamphoefner, Helbich, and Sommer, *News from the Land of Freedom*, p. 91.

81. Quoted in Kamphoefner, Helbich, and Sommer, *News from the Land of Freedom*, p. 271.

82. Quoted in Leslie Corn, "New York State Supreme Court Naturalization Records in the New York County Clerk's Office/Division of Old Records, from the Colonial Period Through 1924," *New York Genealogical and Biographical Society Newsletter*, Winter 2000. www.nygbs.org/info/articles/NYS_naturalizations2.html.

83. Quoted in Kamphoefner, Helbich, and Sommer *News from the Land of Freedom*, p. 166.

84. Quoted in Kamphoefner, Helbich, and Sommer, *News from the Land of Freedom*, p. 159.

85. Carl H. Miller, "The Rise of the Beer Barons," BeerHistory.com, 1999.

www.beerhistory.com/library/holdings/beerbarons.shtml.

86. Quoted in Richard Zelade's Web Site, "Days of Beer and Pretzels: A Beer-Garden History of Austin," 2001. www.io.com/~xeke/daysof.htm.

87. Carl H. Miller, "We Want Beer: Prohibition and the Will to Imbibe," BeerHistory.com, 2000. www.beerhistory.com/library/holdings/prohibition_1.shtml.

88. Quoted in Kamphoefner, Helbich, and Sommer, *News from the Land of Freedom*, p. 518.

89. Quoted in O'Connor, *The German-Americans*, p. 163.

90. Quoted in World of Quotes.com, "Carl Schurz." www.worldofquotes.com/author/Carl-Schurz/1.

91. Quoted in Adams, *The German-Americans*.

92. Quoted in German Americana, "German-American Soldiers in the U.S. Civil War," 2003. www.serve.com /shea/germusa/civilwar.htm.

93. Quoted in Jeff Kisseloff, *You Must Remember This: An Oral History of Manhattan from the 1890s to World War Two*. San Diego: Harcourt, Brace, Jovanovich, 1989, p. 118.

94. Quoted in Joan Morrison and Charlotte Fox Zabusky, *American Mosaic: The Immigrant Experience in the Words of Those Who Lived It*. New York: E.P. Dutton, 1980, p. 74.

95. William J. Clinton, "German American Day, 1995," U.S. Diplomatic Mission to Germany, 2001. www.usembassy.de/usa/etexts/gal-951006.htm.

Chapter Six: A Powerful Force

96. O'Connor, *The German-Americans*, p. 6.

97. Quoted in O'Connor, *The German-Americans*, p. 277.

98. Quoted in O'Connor, *The German-Americans*, p. 372.

99. Richard A. Wright, "Stutz Cars Helped Put the Roar in the Roaring Twenties," *Detroit News*, January 2, 2001. http://info.detnews.com/joyrides/story/index.cfm?id=147.

100. Quoted in Horst G. Denk and Kenneth Rush, "Final Report of the Presidential Commission for the German-American Tricentennial to the President and Congress of the United States," U.S. Diplomatic Mission to Germany, 1983. www.usembassy.de/usa/etexts/ga-tricentennialreport.htm.

101. Quoted in O'Connor, *The German-Americans*, p. 74.

102. Quoted in O'Connor, *The German-Americans*, p. 268.

103. Iowa Health and Physical Readiness Alliance, "Early Gymnastics in America," 2004. www.ihpra.org/gymnastics%20history.htm.

Chapter Seven: "Foreign Malcontents and Misfits"

104. O'Connor, *The German-Americans*, p. 366.

105. Roger O'Conner, "Nativism in the 1890s," Bowling Green State University, 1996. www.bgsu.edu/departments/acs/1890s/ellisisland/nativism1.html.

106. Quoted in O'Connor, *The German-Americans*, p. 122.

107. Quoted in Adams, *The German-Americans*.

108. Quoted in O'Connor, *The German-Americans*, p. 321.

109. Carl Smith, "The Dramas of Haymarket," Chicago Historical Society, 2004. www.chicagohistory.org/dramas/act3/act3.htm.

110. Quoted in O'Connor, *The German-Americans*, p. 381.

111. Quoted in O'Connor, *The German-Americans*, p. 382.

112. Quoted in Mitchel Yockelson, "The War Department: Keeper of Our Nation's Enemy Aliens During World War I," Brigham Young University, April 1998. www.lib.byu.edu/~rdh/wwi/comment/yockel.htm.

113. Quoted in Kisseloff, *You Must Remember This*, p. 118.

114. Quoted in Jean Bethke Elshtain, "Sovereignty at Century's End," 1998. http://sacred-sovereign.uchicago.edu/jbe-sovereignty.html.

115. Severts on the Web, "The German Americans," 2004. www.theseverts.net/German.htm.

116. Aileen Lampel Novick, "Memories of Ridgewood," October 25, 2003. www.gottschee.de/forum/messages/81.html.

117. Quoted in Ursula Vogt Potter, "The Misplaced American," Freedom of Information Times, 2002. www.foitimes.com/internment/Vogt.htm.

118. Quoted in Kamphoefner, Helbich, and Sommer, *News from the Land of Freedom*, p. 516.

Chapter Eight: Remembering a Proud Heritage

119. O'Connor, *The German-Americans*, p. 457.

120. Quoted in Ellen Chrismer, "Lodian Travels to Return to His Russian German Roots," *Lodi News-Sentinel*, March 4, 1997. www.lib.ndsu.nodak.edu/grhc/outreach/journey/newspaper/chrismer.html.

121. Ronald Reagan, "Tricentennial Anniversary Year of German Settlement in America by the President of the United States of America," U.S. Diplomatic Mission to Germany, January 20, 1983. www.usembassy.de/usa/etexts/ga5-830120.htm.

122. Quoted in the German Embassy Online, "Heritage: 300 Years of German Roots in America," October 6, 2003. www.germany-info.org/relaunch/culture/ger_americans/paper.html.

123. Quoted in Echo Germanica, "Bush to Proclaim German American Day," October 2003. www.echoworld.com/B03/B0310/B0310G-ADay.htm.

FOR FURTHER READING

Books

Irene M. Franck, *The German-American Heritage*. New York: Facts On File, 1989. This book explores German immigration from the 1600s into the twentieth century.

Marj Gurasich, *Letters to Oma: A Young German Girl's Account of Her First Year In Texas, 1847*. Fort Worth: Texas Christian University Press, 1989. Firsthand account of a young German immigrant's experiences in Texas.

Dorothy and Thomas Hoobler, *The German American Family Album*. New York: Oxford University Press, 1996. This work includes period photos as well as selections from diaries, letters, memoirs, and newspapers that bring the immigrant experience vividly to life.

Thomas Schouweiler, *Germans in America*. Minneapolis: Lerner, 1994. A good overview of German American history, culture, and contributions.

John D. Zug and Karin Gottier, eds., *German American Life: Recipes and Tra-* *ditions*. Iowa City: Penfield Press, 1991. Covers a variety of topics including German American history, German holiday traditions, and German foods.

Web Sites

German-American History and Heritage (www.germanheritage.com). This site provides biographies, online books, essays, a list of German American organizations, and other information.

Immigration: The Living Mosaic of People, Culture, and Hope (http://library.thinkquest.org/20619/index.html). This site includes articles on U.S. immigrants from Germany, Italy, Ireland, and other countries as well as the history of the Statue of Liberty and Ellis Island. A timeline is also included.

iRhine.com (www.irhine.com). This Web site covers many aspects of the historic Cincinnati neighborhood. It provides a map, updates on community affairs, history, and other details.

WORKS CONSULTED

Books

Howard B. Furer, ed., *The Germans in America: 1607–1970*. Dobbs Ferry, NY: Oceana, 1973. This chronology of German Americans includes a variety of period documents covering various aspects of the German American experience.

Oscar Handlin, *A Pictorial History of Immigration*. New York: Crown, 1972. This photographic history of immigration includes chapters on the Atlantic crossing; early immigration; the specific experiences of German, Italian, Chinese, and other immigrants; and immigration during the twentieth century.

Theodore Huebener, *The Germans in America*. Philadelphia: Chilton, 1962. A history of German American immigration from colonial times until 1960.

Walter D. Kamphoefner, Wolfgang Helbich, and Ulrike Sommer, eds., *News from the Land of Freedom: German Immigrants Write Home*. Ithaca, NY: Cornell University Press, 1988. A collection of letters written by nineteenth-century immigrants to their families in Germany. Gives a multitude of interesting details into the lives of farmers, workers, and domestic servants.

Jeff Kisseloff, *You Must Remember This: An Oral History of Manhattan from the 1890s to World War Two*. San Diego: Harcourt, Brace, Jovanovich, 1989. A compilation of first-person accounts of life in Manhattan during the first part of the twentieth century.

Joan Morrison and Charlotte Fox Zabusky, *American Mosaic: The Immigrant Experience in the Words of Those Who Lived It*. New York: E.P. Dutton, 1980. Immigrants from a variety of countries, including Germany, recall their experiences in coming to America.

Richard O'Connor, *The German-Americans: An Informal History*. Boston: Little, Brown, 1968. A complete and well-written account of the German American experience.

Charles Rounds, *Wisconsin Authors and Their Works*. Madison, Wisconsin: The Parker Educational Company, 1918. An anthology of diverse articles by authors from or about Wisconsin.

Philip Taylor, *The Distant Magnet: European Emigration to the U.S.A.* New York: Harper and Row, 1971. This work details the immigrant experience, including conditions in Europe, the transatlantic voyage, their arrival in America, and how they assimilated.

Doris Weatherford, *Foreign and Female: Immigrant Women in America, 1840–1930*. New York: Schocken, 1986. This book provides detailed accounts of immigrant women's lives drawn from diaries and letters.

Gerald Wilk, *Americans from Germany*. New York: German Information Center, 1976. A collection of brief biographies of successful German American immigrants, including John Jacob Astor, Albert Einstein, Charles Steinmetz, and Levi Strauss.

Internet Sources

Willi Paul Adams, *The German Americans: An Ethnic Experience*, Indiana University–Purdue University. www-lib. iupui.edu/kade/adams/toc.html.

American Park Network, "Statue of Liberty National Monument History: The Immigrant Journey," 2001. www. americanparknetwork.com/parkinfo/sl/ history/journey.html.

William Bell, "Letters from Perth, Upper Canada: Letter IV," Lanark County Genealogical Society, 2004. http://global genealogy.com/LCGS/articles/A-HINT04.HTM.

Carol Gohsman Bowen, ed., "Emigration from Hamburg," Mecklenburg WorldGen-Web, 2001. http://blacklake.biz/meck/ hambrg.htm.

Moritz Bromme, "The Worker Moritz Bromme Describes His Family's Living Conditions," 1905, ZUM-Internet. www. zum.de/psm/dormann/dormann45e.php.

Butler Co. NEGenWeb, "Roots, Branches and Twigs—History of the Family Melvin D. Frahm," 1999. www. rootsweb.com/~nebutler/frahm.html.

Ellen Chrismer, "Lodian Travels to Return to His Russian German Roots," *Lodi News-Sentinel*, March 4, 1997. www.lib. ndsu.nodak.edu/grhc/outreach/journey/ newspaper/chrismer.html.

City of St. Louis, "Peopling St. Louis: the Immigrant Experience," http:// stlouis.missouri.org/government/ heritage/history/immigrant.bak.

William J. Clinton, "German American Day, 1995," U.S. Diplomatic Mission to Germany, 2001. www.usembassy.de/ usa/etexts/gal-951006.htm.

Else Conrad, "Else Conrad on the Living Conditions of Workers' Families in Muenchen," 1909, ZUM-Internet. www. zum.de/psm/dormann/dormann46e.php.

Leslie Corn, "New York State Supreme Court Naturalization Records in the New York County Clerk's Office/Division of Old Records, from the Colonial Period Through 1924," *New York Genealogical and Biographical Society Newsletter*, Winter 2000. www.nygbs.org/info/articles/NYS_ naturalizations2.html.

Daughters of the American Revolution, "About Peter Minuit," 2004. www.molsk. com/dar/minuit.html.

Horst G. Denk and Kenneth Rush, "Final Report of the Presidential Commission for the German-American Tricentennial to the President and Congress of the United States," U.S. Diplomatic Mission to Germany, 1983. www.usembassy.de/usa/etexts/ ga-tricentennialreport.htm.

Echo Germanica, "Bush to Proclaim German American Day," October 2003. www.echoworld.com/B03/B0310/ B0310G-ADay.htm.

Jean Bethke Elshtain, "Sovereignty at Century's End," 1998. http://sacred-sovereign. uchicago.edu/jbe-sovereignty.html.

German Americana, "German-American Soldiers in the U.S. Civil War," 2003. www.serve.com/shea/germusa/civilwar .htm.

———, "The German 1848 Revolution: A German Perspective," January 2, 1997. www.serve.com/shea/germusa/perspekt.htm.

German Embassy Online, "Heritage: 300 Years of German Roots in America," October 6, 2003. www.germany-info.org/ relaunch/culture/ger_americans/paper.html.

Timothy J. Hatton, "The Age of Mass Migration: What We Can and Can't Explain," Kingston University, 1999. http://ecocomm.anu.edu.au/people/info/hatton/Kingston.pdf.

Jeff Hoffman, "Putting Down Roots." www.jeffhoffman.net/roots.htm.

Iowa Health and Physical Readiness Alliance, "Early Gymnastics in America," 2004. www.ihpra.org/gymnastics%20history.htm.

iRhine.com, "History of Over-the-Rhine: The Neighborhood," 2004. www.irhine.com/index.jsp?page=history_neighborhood5.

Lois Jones, "To America," Cochems/Zens Family History, December 2002. www.cochems.com/history/ch8_to_america.html.

Charles F. Kerchner Jr., "Pennsylvania Dutch Are of German Heritage, Not Dutch," C. F. Kerchner & Associates, 2003. www.kerchner.com/padutch.htm.

Barbara Krasner-Khait, "If Not Through New York, Then Where?" Family Chronicle, May/June 1999. http://familychronicle.com/NotThroughNY.html.

Laura Laubeová, "Melting Pot vs. Ethnic Stew," Tolerance, 1999. www.tolerance.cz/default.htm.

Roger D. Launius, "Wernher von Braun (1912–1977)," Sputnik Biographies, 2003. www.hq.nasa.gov/office/pao/History/sputnik/braun.html.

Carl H. Miller, "The Rise of the Beer Barons," BeerHistory.com, 1999. www.beerhistory.com/library/holdings/beerbarons.shtml.

———, "We Want Beer: Prohibition and the Will to Imbibe," BeerHistory.com, 2000. www.beerhistory.com/library/holdings/prohibition_1.shtml.

National Park Service, "The First Gateway—Castle Garden, Ellis Island and Westward Expansion," January 1992. www.nps.gov/jeff/castle_garden.html.

Aileen Lampel Novick, "Memories of Ridgewood," October 25, 2003. www.gottschee.de/forum/messages/81.html.

Roger O'Conner, "Nativism in the 1890s," Bowling Green State University, 1996. www.bgsu.edu/departments/acs/1890s/ellisisland/nativism1.html.

Ohio State University Libraries, "Thomas Nast Portfolio," 2002. www.lib.ohio-state.edu/cgaweb/nast/santa_camp.htm.

Francis Daniel Pastorius, "Pastorius's Description of Pennsylvania, 1700," Early Americas Digital Archive, 2004. www.mith2.umd.edu:8080/eada/html/display.jsp?docs=pastorius_description.xml&action=show.

Ursula Vogt Potter, "The Misplaced American," Freedom of Information Times, 2002. www.foitimes.com/internment/Vogt.htm.

Raymond K. Cunningham Jr. Web Site, "Beware of Spies and Alien Enemies," *Los Angeles Times*, January 6, 1918. http://netfiles.uiuc.edu/rcunning/www/01061801.htm.

Ronald Reagan, "Tricentennial Anniversary Year of German Settlement in America by the President of the United States of America," U.S. Diplomatic Mission to Germany, January 20, 1983. www.usembassy.de/usa/etexts/ga5-830120.htm.

Gerhard Rempel, "The Thirty-Years War," Western New England College, 2000. http://mars.acnet.wnec.edu/~grempel/courses/wc2/lectures/30yearswar.html.

Richard Zelade's Web Site, "Days of Beer and Pretzels: A Beer-Garden History of Austin," 2001. www.io.com/~xeke/daysof.htm.

San Antonio Conservation Society, "King William Area," 2004. www.saconservation.org/tours/sitevisits_kingwilliam. htm.

Miranda Santucci, "An American Patchwork Quilt," American Immigration Law Foundation, 2003. www.ailf.org/awards/2003CelebrateAmerica.asp.

Scriptorium, "Germans Helped Build America—and How Has America Repaid Them?" 2004. www.wintersonnenwende.com/scriptorium/english/archives/germanamerica/ghba03.html.

Severts on the Web, "The German Americans," 2004. www.theseverts.net/German.htm.

Carl Smith, "The Dramas of Haymarket," Chicago Historical Society, 2004. www.chicagohistory.org/dramas/act3/act3.htm.

Spartacus Educational, "German Immigration," 2002. www.spartacus.schoolnet.co.uk/USAEgermany.htm.

———, "Journey to America," 2002. www.spartacus.schoolnet.co.uk/USAEjourney.htm.

Sylvia Payne Higgins Web Site, "Castle Garden," *New York Times*, December 23, 1866. http://genealogy.about.com/gi/dynamic/offsite.htm?site=http%3A%2F%2Fmembers.tripod.com %2F%7ESilvie%2FCastleGarden.html.

Travel Guide to San Antonio Texas, "Top Attractions in San Antonio, Texas," 2002. www.travelto-sanantonio.com/06_attractions03_top.shtml.

University of Waterloo, "1832 Emigrants Handbook for Arrivals at Quebec," 2003. http://ist.uwaterloo.ca/~marj/genealogy/emigrants1832.html.

Robert E. Ward, "From Germantown to Cleveland in Historical Perspective," Federation of German American Societies of Greater Cleveland, 2004. www.fogas.org/history4.htm.

World of Quotes.com, "Carl Schurz." www.worldofquotes.com/author/Carl-Schurz/1.

Richard A. Wright, "Stutz Cars Helped Put the Roar in the Roaring Twenties," *Detroit News*, January 2, 2001. http://info.detnews.com/joyrides/story/index.cfm?id=147.

Mitchel Yockelson, "The War Department: Keeper of Our Nation's Enemy Aliens During World War I," Brigham Young University, April 1998. www.lib.byu.edu/~rdh/wwi/comment/yockel.htm.

Richard H. Zeitlin, "Germans in Wisconsin," State Historical Society of Wisconsin, 1977. http://home.dwave.net/~dhuehner/germanwis.html.

INDEX

PICTURE CREDITS

Cover photo:© Michael T. Sedam/CORBIS

© AKG-Images, 16
© Alfred Stieglitz/George Eastman House/Getty Images, 29
© Bettmann/CORBIS, 14, 18, 26, 36, 51, 56, 59, 61, 63, 66, 67, 70, 72, 81, 84, 87
© Black Star/Alamy, 95
© Chuck Savage/CORBIS, 7
© CORBIS, 24, 28, 44, 49, 63, 81
© David J. and Janice L. Frent Collection /CORBIS, 78
© Jacob A. Riis/Museum of the City of New York/Getty Images, 74, 76
© Kelly-Mooney Photography/CORBIS, 93
© Library of Congress, 22, 33, 34, 38, 41, 55, 58
© Library of Congress/Getty Images, 19
© Photos.com, 12, 91
Ralph Morse/ Time Life Pictures /Getty Images, 88
© Scheufler Collection/CORBIS, 45
Steve Zmina, 8, 12, 91, 94

About the Author

Diane Yancey lives in the Pacific Northwest with her husband, Michael; their dog, Gelato; and their cat, Newton. She has written more than twenty-five books for middle-grade and high-school readers, including *Life During the Roaring Twenties*, *Al Capone*, and *Life in the Dust Bowl*.